FOREWORD by Fred Rogers

Campus cards are not a new idea. Students have had ID cards for years, and colleges and universities have sought to expand the functionality of those cards beyond mere identification. Meal plans, library cards and athletic passes are some of the most common additional uses. Other applications include parking and building access, vending machines, and copying machines. In collaboration with commercial partners in recent years, institutions have added telephone credit cards and ATM banking card functionality to their basic student ID card. Newer uses now under discussion include "smart chip" technology for multiple balances and off-line purchases, medical records, computer security, electronic signatures, bus and transit passes, and use by off-campus merchants, just to name a few. Underlying all of this is the basic student ID card, typically with a picture and some identification number.

How should campuses consider these alternatives and what goals are realistic? How are the goals of the student, the institution, and the card user to be reconciled? This book aims to address those concerns by exploring possible uses and many actual experiences, and by explaining emerging technologies and regulatory issues. Some student card programs seem to be focused on making a lot of money while others seek to discover ways of collapsing multiple, competing on-campus cards into one, simple program. But achieving these larger goals is difficult, due mainly to the differing, sometimes competing objectives of the various users and the realities of the marketplace. Most campus card constituents can agree on the following: They want a card solution that is low in cost, high in fuctionality, secure, and, of course, simple.

The National Association of College and University Business Officers (NACUBO) and the National Association of Campus Card Users (NACCU) have helpfully cooperated to produce this book, addressed to the campus business officer and card office manager or others wanting to explore and understand these important issues and opportunities. There are many places to begin, but on each campus the unique circumstances and history of campus cards and campus card uses make it important for everyone involved to be informed and realistic as they approach the questions of change and improvement. Hopefully, this book will enable or stimulate such informed discussions and lead to even more innovation and service to students in the years to come.

Fred Rogers is the vice-president of university strategy and partnership, Student Advantage, Inc. Previously, he has served as CFO of Carnegie Mellon University and Cornell University, as chairman of the NACUBO Financial Management Committee, and as a board member and treasurer of EACUBO.

ACKNOWLEDGMENTS

The author is deeply indebted to a number of people for their kind assistance in the preparation of this book. I hope I will not omit anyone who helped me during the months it took me to write it. It is worth sharing how this book came about in the first place, in helping to understand where one finds inspiration.

The need for a book on campus cards came to my attention when I attended the 21st Century Executive Symposium, sponsored by NACUBO and KPMG earlier this year in Washington, D.C. I heard speakers talk about campus cards, how efficient they are, how they provide added security to entry, and serve as "firewalls." Then, I read Bill Gates's latest book, *Business @ the Speed of Thought.* Gates writes about changing technology, new expectations, and more specifically about how smart cards will make the use of digital information pervasive.

Armed with this newfound information, I approached my supervisor, Donna Klinger, director of publications for the National Association of College and University Business Officers. Donna reminded me that NACUBO had just offered a workshop on campus cards and that Joseph G. Pietrantoni, associate vice president for auxiliary services, Duke University, had written a feature article in the January 1999 issue of NACUBO's magazine, BUSINESS OFFICER, titled "Getting on the Bandwidth." With my strong background in information technology and having written seven technology-related books, I expressed my interest in putting a book together for NACUBO on card technology.

At that time, February 2000, Donna gave me the assignment to discuss my idea with Lyn White, then the executive director of the National Association of Campus Card Users (NACCU), while at their annual conference in San Jose, California, March 11 to 14, 2000. I attended the San Jose meeting armed with a book chapter outline. At the meeting I began my information gathering for the proposed campus card book. Lunch with NACCU Board member, Shirley Everson, brought further momentum when Shirley promised to present the idea to the board that very day. Word came back that the board approved the book idea, and I was off and running.

My approach to technical writing has always been to write in clear, laymen's terms while maintaining the interest of the experts. I soon discovered that no book on the subject, covering more than 40 years of card history, existed. Therefore, I had the additional challenge of breaking new ground.

My next step was to attend the CardTech/SecurTech conference, May 1 to 4, 2000, in Miami Beach, Florida. Here, I found lots of B2B (business-to-business) happening along with every presenter speaking in acronyms. It sounded like a foreign language! Cards with a chip (magnetic memory cards) were being highly touted in the large exhibition hall with 303 exhibitors and 8,500 attendees.

After discussions with many experts in the field, and upon completion of this book, I can now clearly state that this is a technology that can be either simple or

Campus Cards: Making an Informed Decision

National Association of College and
University Business Officers
Washington, DC
www.nacubo.org

Printed in the United States of America

———————————————

Design by Lynn Riley

Editor, Karen Bandy

Production Manager, Judith Castagna

Publications Director, Donna Klinger

ISBN 1-56972-015-0

SPONSOR:
Student Advantage

Through its SA Cash program, Student Advantage is working with Campus Card program offices around the country to extend the benefits of value and convenience that their students enjoy on campus to the off-campus merchants appropriate to their campus. We are proud to sponsor a book on this significant subject and hope that it serves the campus managers well as they seek to address these important issues and opportunities.

CO-SPONSOR: iCollege

iCollege is a nationally recognized leader in the areas of Internet services, card system software and technology, custom publishing, and reprographics. iCollege understands campus needs and we can successfully introduce and customize new applicatons to keep you at the forefront of technology. iCollege's mission is to provide top quality products and services to enable your campus to maintain its all-important academic focus.

CO-SPONSOR: Schlumberger

Schlumberger Smart Campus Access Solution provides an end-to-end suite of smart cards, terminals, software, and professional services that seamlessly integrates advanced network security, campus auxiliary services, and on- and off-campus merchant applications. The Schlumberger Smart Campus Access Solution delivers a solid source of value-added benefit, as well as cost savings and security that brings added efficiencies through its integrated architecture.

and these donors:

> AT&T CAMPUSWIDE
> IDENTATRONICS
> PNC BANK
> SCAN TECHNOLOGY
> WILLIAM EXLINE COMPANY
> VINGCARD PERSONA

complicated. Going from an ID card to a card with a chip is a quantum leap. Most U.S. colleges and universities find the magnetic stripe or multiple stripes and bar-code on a card serve all their needs. Chip technology is something to review, but the higher costs to produce the so-called "smart cards" requires serious justification. Factor in efficiency of your system. Talk to managers of card offices that have a system that is close to what you envision; learn what is good and not so good about their systems. With a strong infrastructure in the U.S., including telephone networks, and the Internet, colleges and universities are not moving as quickly into card chip technology as elsewhere in the world. Make an informed decision.

There are many people I would like to thank for helping to make this book a reality. First, a small army of reviewers went over the "draft" with a fine hand, providing their extensive knowledge and experience. These reviewers included: Tom Hawk, vice president of planning and finance at the Community of College of Philadelphia; Joe Pietrantoni, associate vice president for auxiliary services, at Duke University; Tom Bell, executive director, auxiliary services, SUNY Geneseo; Ron Pierce, executive director of NACCU; Tim Aaron, vice president of iCollege; Stephanie Woodfork, program manager for NACUBO; and Fred Rogers, vice president of Student Advantage.

I would also like to thank Kelly Scherer of Oregon State University who provided a valuable sample of their RFP in the Appendix, and Ralph McCaughan, Associate University Counsel in the Office of Counsel of Duke University, who provided his *Outline of Selected Regulation E Provisions*. (See Appendix.)

Donna Klinger brought sense and sensibility to the book with such comments as, "Has this been defined? What did they do? Don't leave me hanging. Transition?" Thank you, Donna, for your effective edit, and for keeping me pointed on course.

Certainly, Lyn White, helped give this book a strong launch and provided her wealth of knowledge, based on her years of experience in the field of card technology, starting with the University of Florida, where she pioneered the university's Gator 1 Card program, and her years as executive director of the National Association of Campus Card Users.

Judith Castagna, NACUBO's production manager, performs miracles. This book was rushed through the design, typesetting, and printing process by her in record time. Five stars to Judy!

My beloved son, Lt. George G. Grills, now a graduate student at the University of Massachusetts, and in service to the U.S. Coast Guard, shared with me the usefulness of the campus one-card at the University of Massachusetts at Amherst, which led to its inclusion as one of the 10 "Profiles" in this book. Thanks, George, and thanks to Linda Overing of the University of Massachusetts at Amherst for providing her campus card profile. I would also like to thank the following for their campus "Profiles:" Jana Gittins of Utah State University; Joseph G. Pietrantoni of Duke University; Shirley Everson of the University of Minnesota; Gary Ricard of Pennsylvania State University; John Beckwith of Loyola Marymont University; Ruben Rivera of Colby College; Suellyn Hull of the University of Arizona; Bob Russell of the University of Michigan; and Joan Hammer of the College of Wooster.

And last, I would like to thank my dear friend, Col. Mike Harris, Ret., for his encouragement and humor during the process of getting this book completed.

Caroline M. Grills
Washington, D.C., November 2000

CONTENTS

CHAPTER 6

Security 57

- Access Control
- Securing E-Commerce
- Physical Security with Campus "One-Card" Systems
- ID and Beyond
- Security

CHAPTER 7

Sorting Out Cards, Politics, and Compliance 67

- Smart and Not-As-Smart Cards
- Politics
- Compliance and "Reg. E"

CHAPTER 8

Toward Standardization 75

- Steps Toward Standardization
- Existing Standards
- Standards Under Development
- Entities Driving Standards

CHAPTER 9

Migration to Multiapplication Platforms 83

- Health Care Applications
- Bank Relationships and Off-Campus Merchants
- Smart Chips
- Summary

CHAPTER 10

Tomorrow's Opportunities 93

- What's Next?
- Smart Card Life Cycle
- Yesterday, Today, and Tomorrow
- Going Global

CHAPTER 1

Introduction to the Card Industry

- Introduction
- Technology Defined and Redefined
- An Enabling Technology
- A Bridge to Information and Cyberspace

This book is organized to help both the newcomer to campus card technology as well as the experienced card office manager/director to move forth and make an informed decision. As we begin our endeavor, let one and all profit from the experience of campus card experts. They want you to plan every step of the way, get senior management's support and enthusiasm, and to understand that keeping the system simple to start with will make life easier for all concerned.

Introduction

Ever since the invention and development of the plastic card, over two thirds of the existing 3,614 colleges and universities in the U.S. have implemented card systems for use on their campuses.[1]

Originally, in the early 1960s, campus cards were used only for identification purposes—for student events, in libraries, and for dining entry. Later, specific uses evolved where cards could allow record keeping for payment purposes. Some examples include payment for laundry, meals, and copiers. Now, such cards are on campuses all over the world and are used by millions of students. The size of the market is tremendous and growing.

Today, campus cards range from the simple identification (ID) card, to the magnetic stripe card with or without the addition of a barcode, to "smart cards" (with an embedded electronic chip). The card with single or multiple magnetic stripes and perhaps a barcode is the card most commonly found on campuses in the United States. These cards are solidly in place on U.S. campuses because they are economical, they serve most, if not all, campus needs; and they use the same technology as other cards used throughout the U.S. economy. Currently, less than two percent of college campuses in the United States use "smart cards."

Regardless of the type of technology used, cards that serve multiple functions (and are often called "all-campus cards" or "campus one-cards") have taken over as the card of choice on many campuses. An all-campus card provides:

Cost savings

Administrative efficiencies

Improved campus image, and

New revenue streams

Figure 1.
Some Different Types of Campus Cards

Simple ID Card

Card with a stripe

Card with multiple stripes

Card with barcode

Card with stripe (or stripes) and barcode

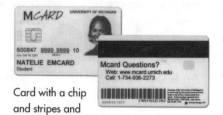

Card with a chip and stripes and perhaps a barcode

Without a doubt, campus cards have made life easier for all who use them, especially in the business management of a college or university. Cards are an excellent solution to managing data, money, security, identification, and other applications. However, implementing a campus card system requires planning and strategizing. It is not a quick panacea. The key to an effective campus card system is thorough short- and long-range planning before implementing a system.

Jack Mapes, sales and marketing manager for Schlumberger, Campus Systems Group, presents an excellent business model for a successful card program. [2]

A Successful Card Program

Is Convenient to Cardholder	Easy to load value
	Easy to understand
	Easy to use
Is Affordable	Return on investment
	Generates revenue
Offers Growth Potential	Expandable for future uses
	Project investment

As the card industry is an evolving industry—with an evolving technology—planning should include provision for decision-making that allows for change. Managers need to plan strategically. Every so often, a technological change comes along that offers much better ways of doing things. Thus far, the campus cards have adjusted and moved transitionally along with the technology. Some call cards "the killer app of the future." The fact is campus cards are very much in the here and now.

Technology Defined and Redefined

The original campus card technology was simple in its applications, management, and cost. With changes in technology, the campus card system has grown to major proportions. For example, at Duke University, there are 300,000 on-campus transactions with Duke's all-campus card each day and the strategic plan calls for expansion up to 500,000 daily transactions by 2002. The existing 900 readers and point-of-sale (POS) devices at Duke will increase to over 2,000. The total cost of the installed system at Duke is in the $1.6 million range, and annual dollars transacted there are $20 million. Card technology continues to redefine itself to match the needs of other information technologies. One of the major uses of campus cards is as a way of managing payments within the college or university community.

Receivables Management

Use of plastic cards for electronic payments is now common throughout the U.S. economy, and this has also become one of the major uses for campus cards as well. Electronic payment systems, using plastic payment cards, is a strong receivables management option for colleges and universities. Payment cards offer a fast, convenient, safe way to be paid. Like all forms of payment, plastic payment cards have direct and indirect costs. These costs will make payment a more or less attractive option for each institution—depending on how the card program is implemented. [3]

There are five main categories of payment cards:

Credit cards. This is the most common type of payment card in the United States. Credit cards allow cardholders to pay their balance in full at the end of the billing period (usually monthly) or revolve the balance into a line of credit.

Debit cards. These cards access the cardholder's demand deposit account (DDA) or checking account directly. Debit cards may be "on line," requiring a personal identification number (PIN) or "off-line," and processed like a credit card.

Charge cards. The total amount charged on the account ID due at the close of the billing period, usually one month.

Commercial cards. These cards, issued to businesses, corporations, government agencies, and colleges and universities, are used to improve cash management and reduce purchasing costs.

Cash cards or prepaid cards. These are cards that have preloaded cash value either embedded in a chip or encoded on a magnetic stripe on the card. Alternatively, these cards may be linked to a prepaid account that is debited when a transaction is processed.

> **In developing your own campus card system, look at individual needs, the capability of staff, current systems (that might profit by the introduction of a card), and cost to implement and run the card system.**

In each payment card transaction, there are the same four roles: the cardholder; the financial institution that issues the card; the seller of the goods or services; and the seller's card processor, sometimes called an acquirer. The other players are the card associations, Visa and MasterCard, and independent companies such as American Express, Diner's Club, or Discover.

Figure 2.

U. of Pennsylvania Visa Card

The campus card is usually more than just a payment card. To successfully implement a card system today, each institution needs to develop the system that matches the needs of the college or university. In developing your own campus card system, look at individual needs, the capability of staff, current systems (that might profit by the introduction of a card), and cost to implement and run the card system.

Also as technology is evolving, changing, and even converting very rapidly, one must stay abreast of the technology, considering whether to have open or closed architecture, deciding who will be systems providers, and deciding whether to use on-line or off-line applications. You will need to develop technology partnerships on- and off-campus.

An Enabling Technology

One of the benefits of the campus card is its portability. A typical polyvinyl chloride (PVC) plastic card measures 2.125 inches by 3.375 inches with a thickness of 0.031 (nom.) inches. As we all know, plastic cards can be carried easily in a wallet. Furthermore, campus cards are complementary and compatible with other technologies. There will be more about this in ensuing chapters. We can view campus cards as an enabling tool—a card can go almost anywhere and will soon be able to do almost anything.

Think about how campus cards might have a direct impact on your college or university. Joseph G. Pietrantoni, associate vice president for Auxiliary Services at Duke University and a pioneer in campus cards, suggests you begin planning your campus card system by asking:
- Do we want to manage and control privitization vendor activity?
- Do we want customers to review their account balance at the time the transaction occurs?
- Do we want to ensure that loss of the card does not cause a loss of the remaining funds on the card?
- Do we want a quick and easy process for deactivating a card?
- Do we want the card manufacturing and replacement to be low in cost?

Some Business Models

Before embarking on a campus card system, Tim Aaron, vice president of iCollege, Campus Card Systems, recommends having "Two strategic missions using both an Internal focus and an External focus.

Internal focus: To unite various departments or systems to a single card, and promote the card as a "service" that supports functions on campus.

External focus: To see revenue-generating opportunities off-campus, such as calling card, banking, and community businesses.

Eventually, most campuses will end up with a mix of internal and external business. Aaron further advises, "Start out focused internally then expand out once you've got 'your ducks in order.' "

From a business perspective, the campus card makes money and it saves money. Here are some examples:

- Campus cards make money by providing a handy, easy-to-use card for the purpose of bookstore use, for vending machines, laundry, and photocopiers.
- Campus cards make money by providing quick access to distance learning.
- Campus cards save money by providing an easy tracking tool for financial transactions, dining hall and dorm access.
- Campus cards save money by tracking parking and transit.
- Campus cards make money by affinity programs with off-campus merchant sponsors.
- Campus cards make money by connecting students to ticketed events and activities.
- Campus cards save money by maintaining secure access applications such as Intranet networks.

Furthermore, campus cards to support security systems can reduce property damage and loss. (See chapter 6 on Security.)

A Bridge to Information and Cyberspace

Most campuses today use simple, low-cost magnetic stripe cards, but the card with a chip ("smart card") is growing in use. The smart card offers even more opportunities for making transactions or giving users convenient access to information and services. For example, today, many U.S. students carry wireless phones. In Europe, a smart card can be inserted into a slot in a wireless phone. This allows the smart card user to:

Order air, train, or bus ticketless travel
Access personal medical information
Order via the Internet or from catalogs
Order textbooks
Access distance learning
Use on-line campus services
Engage in various kinds of E-commerce

Is this future technology? One answer is yes, on most U.S. campuses. However, in Europe and other parts of the world, smart cards have been in use since the early 1980s. According to the International Card Manufacturers Association, over 1.5 billion smart cards are in use throughout the world. These cards with a chip are used for public transportation, gate control, pay and display meters, ticketless entry, Internet security, virtual access, digital certificates, and secure E-mail. This means service, anytime and anywhere.

Presently, about 40 college and university campuses in the United States are planning or have implemented smart card systems. The smart card promises more diverse applications, benefiting students and institutions alike, as will be discussed in greater detail in later chapters.

Smart cards are much more expensive than cards with a magnetic stripe or a barcode. Nevertheless, the U.S. federal government is moving rapidly into the world of smart, chip-based cards. By the end of 2000, the General Services Administration (GSA) will have issued 4 million chip-based ID cards for the Department of Defense (DOD). The U.S. Navy is developing software and hardware to be used with smart cards functioning as a "key" to access information faster, more conveniently, and in a secure manner. The U.S. Army is also developing smart cards to store medical information for both its personnel and their dependents.

Cybermark, an organization which specializes in the creation of smart card communities, is currently working with 30 or more college campuses, assisting them in the implementation of smart cards for E-commerce applications. "Smart cards are the link between the virtual world and the brick and mortar world, and I believe now's the time to get on board," says Thomas K. Burke, vice president of marketing at Cybermark. Burke anticipates strong market penetration with 10 to 20 percent of colleges and universities implementing smart cards in the coming years.

As campus cards have evolved from simple ID cards to magnetic/barcode cards, to the most sophisticated state-of-the-art cards with an embedded chip, they have become a true bridge to information and cyberspace. For on- and off-campus business, campus cards are the tool to develop key partnerships with financial institutions and merchants, thereby maximizing college and university revenue potential.

Nancy Blackburn, writing for *Intel-CardNews* magazine, reports that 250,000 California college students at the University of California, Riverside; Pasadena Community College; and the nine-campus Los Angeles Community College district will soon be using smart cards.[4]

Campus cards are versatile. They are an integral part of information technology, being defined and redefined as technology evolves. Now, let's move on to the next chapter to explore the underlying basics of card systems.

REFERENCES
1. White, Lyn, "Campus Card Overview," presentation at the National Association of College and University Business Officers Campus Card Professional Development Program, New Orleans, LA, January 2000.
2. Mapes, Jack, "Redefining the Campus ID, Here and in Cyberspace: It's Not Just A Meal Plan Anymore," presentation at National Association of Campus Card Users (NACCU) 7th Annual Conference, San Jose California, March 12, 2000.
3. *College & University Business Administration*, 6th Edition, Chapter 8, "Treasury Management," National Association of College and University Business Officers, Washington, DC, 2000.
4. Blackburn, Nancy, "Smart cards are here to stay," *Intel-Card News*, May 2000.

CAMPUS CARD PROFILE #1
University of Massachusetts at Amherst "UCard"

The UCard program at the University of Massachusetts at Amherst has been in place since 1997. Current enrollment is approximately 24,000 students and 5,000 faculty and staff. The UCard office is managed by Linda Overing, with two full-time employees and an average of eight student staff members.

The UCard Office operates under the Office of the vice-chancellor of administration and finance and works with all departmental units to support a one-card approach to verification, financial applications, and security. The UCard is used as an identifier, a meal ticket, exterior dorm key, library card, time card, and debit card. Access to recreational facilities and athletic and cultural events requires utilization of the UCard. The debit program includes over 40 campus retail, food, and service locations as well as vending and laundry machines in over 60 buildings. Copier installation is planned for 2001.

The UCard program operation is self-funded. Its start-up costs were financed by a loan from the campus, to be paid back with earnings from interest and debit account transaction fees. The program constantly looks for ways to expand participation and reduce costs; recent initiatives include an on-line deposit feature, on-line debit application, and E-mail statements. Being able to afford to stay current with technology and system enhancements is a challenge.

UMass utilizes the AT&T CampusWide One-Card System, an on-line system with magnetic stripe technology. The UCard also provides a barcode for use by the campus library.

URL: www.umass.edu/ucard

CHAPTER 2

Getting Started

- Goals of a Campus Card System
- Planning Steps for a Card System
- Card Fabrication and Costs
- Card Readers
- Small-to-Large Systems

Depending on the size and scope of the card system you are designing for your campus, it can range from a simple identification card (ID) card to a card with bar codes and/or a single magnetic stripe, to one with multiple stripes, or a smart card with an embedded electronic chip. The technology you choose depends in part on the services you plan to provide now and your vision for the future growth of the card system. Therefore, determining the size and scope is the first step in getting started.

Goals of a Campus Card System

Aiming toward a campus "one-card" system will ensure a card program beneficial to students, faculty, and staff. Ron Pierce, executive director of the National Association of Campus Card Users (NACCU), ranks the following implementation goals and reasons for a "one-card" on your campus.[1]

Convenience. The convenience of having only one card that does a variety of things both on and off campus will allow you to maintain a higher standard of customer service. Keeping your customers happy will keep them coming back to use your services and facilities.

Safety. Students, faculty, and staff will not have to carry cash or write as many checks. There will be less chance of someone using a lost or stolen card. Keeping track of one card is easier than keeping track of three or four cards.

Marketing. You will be able to market your ID card program as a whole, rather than in pieces. One overall campaign from one office will go a long way in helping promote total card usage. Do not forget marketing the card program to faculty and staff, as well as to students. Their support and use will encourage others and help to gain acceptance.

Manageability. With a one-card campus, you will be able to manage all of your assets and programs with greater ease. You won't have to depend on someone else in another office to get you that report you needed yesterday. You will have better control over the entire campus ID program. Of course, with this control comes accountability for the success or failure of the program. But wouldn't you rather have control over your destiny than let someone else control it?

Accountability. We all hear about it every day. What kind of records are you keeping to back up what you are doing? Does the money balance out every day? Did the student enter a location he or she should not have? Door access is an important safety and security factor. When door access security and safety are identified as necessary, you can have a record with a card of who enters and exits a building, and prevent unauthorized people from having building or door access to a secured section of a building. With a one-campus card concept, all of these questions can be answered, and you have the ability to back up your words with documentation.

Operations. With a one-card concept, fewer people are involved from around the campus in ensuring the success of the program. It's easier for one office to handle all or many of the aspects of a one-card program. Students will know where they have to go if they have a problem with their cards. This keeps them from having to guess which office handles what problem. An ideal location for the card office is the college or university Student Center where students can walk-up to a counter to obtain information about the one-card, replace a lost card, or just have a friendly visit.

Statistics. Keep up with four of the five W's as they relate to marketing. With a one-card concept, you can tell *what* facilities or programs were used by *whom, when* they were used, and *where* money was spent. Then, take these four W's and learn *why* college students do the things they do in the context of a one-card program. Understanding *why* gives you the key to developing and marketing new services.

Access. The ability to use this one card to allow controlled access into resident halls, computer labs, and other key locations will help you by allowing only those students who are authorized for a specific location to gain access. Again, the student only has to carry one card that does all of this.

Public relations. With a good one-campus-card program comes recognition from not only your students, but also from your administration and community. Although it is not the only reason to have a successful program, public relations will go a long way in achieving your goals and objectives.

Profit. This is another key word as it relates to the one-card concept. Do you really want to, or have to, make a profit with your card system? Or can you? In some cases, profit is expected from the operations. There are a few ways to generate revenue (replacement cards, off-campus commissions, handling fees), but not necessarily many ways to generate much of a profit. What is the real purpose of your one-card program? Most likely, it is to provide customer service to your students, faculty, and staff. If by some chance you generate a profit, then all the better. Review once again your mission for a campus card system. Your mission might be chiefly service. Therefore, profit should not be your highest priority. In fact, your mission might be looking toward the next generation of your card system for revision, modification, or upgrade. This will probably remove you further from making a profit. On campuses, profit in card systems in not a likely primary goal.

If the smart card technology is affordable on your campus, it can potentially address all the points above and leave room for additional services that will be discussed in chapters 9 and 10. However, the points just listed can also be addressed, at least in the near term, by the less expensive magnetic stripe and barcode technologies currently in use by most colleges and universities. First, develop a strategic plan and then a business plan.

Planning Steps for a Card System

At the most recent NACCU conference in San Jose, California, Tom Barlow of Xavier University and Pam Boykin and Tom Hilton from the CBORD Group defined the basics of producing the small all campus card. Typically, the groundwork, and likely the full management of campus cards should be classified as an "auxiliary function" of the college or university. [2]

NACUBO's book, *College and University Business Administration,* advises "Auxiliary enterprises support the mission of the institution and provide essential services to the campus community of students, faculty, and staff. They are "enterprises" in that they are generally self-supporting, recovering their costs through the fees or prices they charge for their goods and services. Ideally, they may even contribute to the institution's revenue stream. Depending on the operation, they may have special criteria for financial transactions and accounting practices, purchasing, personnel classification, and other items, like their counterparts in the for-profit sector. Typical college and university auxiliary services include food services, student and faculty housing, campus stores, retail sales, vending, conferences, arenas, stadiums, health programs, printing, copying and binding, and laundry services. Campus card systems are frequently utilized in auxiliary enterprises." [3]

Aiming toward a campus "one-card" system will ensure a card program beneficial to students, faculty, and staff.

Before setting up shop, it is necessary to do your homework. Define the scope of the system with analysis and planning; decide upon your objectives or vision, determine your constituencies, and then do a preliminary budget. Everyone will ask, "What is this going to cost?" A preliminary marketing plan will aid greatly in your planning, review the campus infrastructure, and then put an implementation plan in place. The following steps are necessary in setting up your preliminary plans for a card system.[4]

Step 1. Analysis and Planning

All departments that might be involved or affected by the card system should be involved in meetings to define the scope of the system. Discuss what you want to accomplish. Determine what services will be provided—identification, building access, food service accounts, bookstore sales, debit card services, parking lot and transit use, etc. What is your target date to begin distribution of the card?

Step 2. Objectives – Vision

Will the campus card system be centralized or decentralized? Will it use one card or will there be more than one card? Keep it simple. Are you planning for card use only at on-campus locations, or will there be off-campus use as well?

Step 3. Constituencies

Who are your constituencies? They might include: students, staff (faculty and administration), visitors, conferees, alumni, members of the community, and others.

Step 4. Budget

How are you going to pay for this? Will there be partners to share costs? Depending upon the number of students a card system is designed to serve, the cost per card will decrease as the volume of students using the card increases. In estimating card costs, seek the help of vendors and perhaps other colleges and universities with a card system similar to the one you are planning.

For specific costs to set up and run a campus card system, one must draw up a Request For a sample Proposal (RFP) (see Appendix) and contact specific hardware and software vendors for their estimates. Leading campus card vendors and their contact information are listed in the Appendix.

At the iCollege, Campus Card Systems Partners Conference, held in Pittsburgh, Pennsylvania, April 14, 2000, Jim Andersen, Director of Auxiliary Services Business Operations at the University of Wisconsin at Platteville, identified "36 Ways to Finance Your Card Office." Some highlights of possible income sources to consider are:

- Charge a segregated fee. For example, the University of Wisconsin at Platteville charges a $5.00 segregated fee per year per full time equivalent (FTE) for the card office.
- Have departments buy their own equipment and pay for the equipment maintenance.
- Share costs with other departments.

- Share staff, such as Auxiliary Services sharing with the Accounting Office.
- Where cards are used in academic areas, seek academic support.
- Spread costs out to departments that benefit from the system, based on volume or maintenance costs.
- Charge a card activation fee as an automatic add-on to the student's semester bill.
- Make ID badges.
- Since Food Service is usually the major user of the system, include this department in the card office budget.
- If you have copiers that departments use and they need an ID type card, see if you can produce the cards for them for a fee.
- Charge a lost card fee. Such fees vary from $5.00 to $25.00 per lost card.
- Charge a fee to re-encode cards as a preventative measure to stop repeat card re-encoding.
- Mark IDs for camps and conferences.
- Sell advertising space on the back of the card.
- Charge off-campus merchants a fee (usually a percentage of sales) to be connected with your debit card program.
- See if you can apply the vending commission money to the campus card office.
- Establish a relationship with a banking or telecommunications partner. They are sometimes willing to pay a fee and/or guarantee as part of a partnership with the ID card.

These are but a few ideas to stimulate your creative thinking.

Step 5. Marketing

What is your theme? Are you marketing internally, externally, or both? Tell users all about the "what, where, and when" of card use. Show how easy the card is to use. Students can be your best marketers. Students love the technology and the convenience. They would prefer not to carry cash. Freshmen orientation is a great time to introduce the campus card (or cards). Be an entrepreneurial thinker. Every successfully run campus uses cards. Campus cards can be a tool to:

Manage money. Money management should be kept simple with no minimum deposits and no minimum balance to maintain. Making deposits should be easy and convenient. Parents appreciate the convenience of campus cards and find them a great budgeting tool, because they are provided with some control over where their money is being spent. Many incoming students have never maintained a checking account or even written a check, but they know how to use plastic.

Establish a banking relationship. Most campuses go this route.

Pay for Vending. Will vendors fund the card system? Consider ways that vendors can fund the card system, and approach them for their thinking.

Step 6. Review of Campus Infrastructure

Tom Hawk of the Community College of Philadelphia recommends reviewing the campus infrastructure "to determine the extent that it will have to be modified to support a proposed card system." He further recommends addressing such issues as the following: Are the electrical/network requirements in place or accessible? Will security and vending systems require significant modifications to accommodate the card system? Does the existing technology infrastructure support the proposed card applications that will be installed on the campus?[5]

Step 7. Implementation

Staffing the card office is very important. Staff must be able to communicate well with campus administration, faculty, students, parents, and the community. In other words, everyone who comes in contact with the card office should have a positive experience. The card office staff must establish a positive relationship with student leaders who will affirm the campus card's worth. Students should enjoy going to the card office, not dread it.

Card Fabrication and Costs

Card cost is a function of the amount of memory, complexity, and function of the operating system and level of encryption or security required. Whereas magnetic stripe cards generally cost around $0.50, smart cards start at double that amount and most often are in the $2.00 to $10.00 range. You pay for what you get. Cost can be defrayed by advertising on the card, as well as through cosponsorship.[6]

The following specifications are samples from the Oregon State University RFP shown in the Appendix.

- Strong, flexible PVC laminate with finish for direct printing with digital imaging system;

- Dimensions: 2.125" x 3.375" x 0.031" nom.
- Standard American Banking Association (ABA) Track II, high-energy magnetic stripe and encoding, customized to two tracks wide.
- Three tracks is the accepted standard, to allow for off-line door locks.
- Encoding to include field for incremental lost card code.
- Pre-printed on front with 4-color process, 1-color drop-in front.

Card Readers

One or more card readers will be needed at each point-of-sale (POS) or transaction. Systems may be designed to have card readers that communicate with centralized transaction processing software or may have an open architecture that allows use of currently marketed brands of card readers to communicate with the system transaction processing software. Readers can differ greatly. Are they to be used on line or off line, or do they need to be customized for such purposes as laundry.

All card reader models offered (privilege verification, POS, vending, door access, copier, and remote value add-on terminal) must have the following features:

Reader types
Privilege verification
POS, vending
Door access
Copier
Remote value add-on terminal

First develop a strategic plan and then a business plan.

A continuous swipe-through style card slot is required which reads the encoded information on Track II of the ABA magnetic stripe on the ID card (exception for proximity access readers). System communicate with the transaction processor on line and in real time and must be capable of storing a minimum of 1,000 transactions off line, which can be automatically uploaded to the transaction processor upon restoration of communication. It must provide a visual response to operator and cardholder, however, this is not true for some readers, such as smart card vending, which is off line and does not communicate with a transaction processor.

On line versus Off line Considerations

John Beckwith tells how such decisions were made at Loyola Marymount University: "Early in the process, we were able to identify two areas where we could differentiate the need between on line and off line access control; number of users; and frequency of access. For high volume (users and/or access), an on line system is the preferred choice. We have on line access control on the entrances to all our residence halls as well as at many other locations. On line locks are also appropriate where rapid changes or monitoring are required. Alternately, for very low volume, key locks still made sense (cleaning lockers, equipment rooms, etc.) It was the large area in between the low- and high-volume usage that appeared to be a fit for off line locks. Eventually, it also became obvious to us that the number of locks (read "cost") would also play into the decision-making process (installing a thousand on line locks becomes prohibitive)."[7]

Specifications for Card Readers

In your RFP, ask the bidder to provide a diagram detailing your system's communication. Specifically detail how the copier reader communicates with the on-line transaction processor. List which of your card reader models can communicate with the transaction processor across the campus network. Describe how each of your reader models indicates an off-line condition.

The following is a sampling of "specs" when putting out an RFP for card readers:[8]

Door Access Readers:
Bidder is to provide door access readers.
Describe how your access reader control electronics can be mounted, i.e., maximum distance from reader, behind a wall, etc.
Describe how your door access readers provide off-line authorization for access.
Door access application and readers to allow for key override.
Door access readers to support an optional PIN pad.
The institution will install door hardware; bidder will install connections to readers.
Door access readers and recommended hardware are to be compatible with best commercial grade lock mechanisms.

Point-of-Sale (POS) Readers:
full-featured POS readers can report PLU key totals for given date ranges.

Vending Readers:
Describe how your remote value add-on terminal cabinet is tamper resistant, and whether it includes a monitor or alarm to protect deposits.

Portable Card Readers:
Must be able to hold a database of a minimum of 2,500 accounts for activity privilege verification and meal plan or debit/credit plan transactions.
Uploads transactions automatically upon connection to the on-line transaction processor.

In summary, reader types are selected by various configurations, for example:

Access	On line swipe, on line swipe with pin pad. On line proximity, Off line
Point-of-Sale (POS)	Simple medium-to-high end
Vending/Copy/Low end	On line Off line

Small-To-Large Systems

Magnetic stripe. The magnetic stripe card is almost 30 years old, and is used by millions in the U.S. for everything from credit charge cards to grocery store identification. Commonly called the "mag stripe" card, it is in common use on the campuses of the United States.

Bar code. Cards are available with only a bar code, or bar-coded cards may be combined with cards having a magnetic stripe. A popular application for the combination card (bar code plus magnetic stripe) is found in college and university libraries, where users can check out a book themselves by using their campus card containing a bar code and a magnetic stripe.

Smart cards. Smart card chip sets can store large amounts of data, making them ideal for transactions requiring advanced memory and read/write capabilities. The cards' high security prevents unauthorized access to data.[9] Major charge card companies in the U.S. are now introducing their cards with a chip. They are particularly attractive to people who want to do E-commerce on the Internet with high security protection of their personal information. As these cards come into more popular use in the commercial and government sectors, it is just a matter of time until this acceptance crosses over into campus card applications, using either the commercial charge cards or the campus's own "smart card" system.

REFERENCES

1. Pierce, Ron, *"From the Desk of the President,"* Card Talk, National Association of Campus Card Users (NACCU) July/August 2000.
2. Barlow, Tom, Pam Boykin, and Tom Hilton, CBORD Group Gold Corporate Presentation "Small Campus Card Systems," presentation at National Association of Campus Card Users, NACCU Annual Conference, March 11-14, 2000.
3. *College and University Business Administration, Sixth Edition,* Chapter 20 – "Auxiliary Enterprises and Other Activities," National Association of College and University Business Officers, Washington, DC, July 2000.
4. See Reference 2 above.
5. Hawk, Tom, of Community College of Philadelphia, PA. Personal correspondence, October 2000.

6. Aaron, Tomothy S., from *Oregon State University (OSU) Sample RFP* from the presentation, "Partnership Formation: Writing the RFP and Evaluating the Responses," presented at National Association of Campus Card Users, NACCU Annual Conference, March 11-14, 2000.
7. Beckwith, John, *"Planning and Cooperation Are Keys to Offline Locks,"* Card Talk, National Association of Campus Card Users (NACCU) January 2000.
8. Ibid reference 6 above.
9. Urquhart, Bruce, "De-Mystifying Smart Cards," presentation at National Association of Campus Card Users, NACCU, May 2000.

CAMPUS CARD PROFILE #2
Utah State University's USU Card

The USU Card program at Utah State University in Logan, Utah, has been in place since 1990. With current enrollment of approximately 20,000 students and 5,000 faculty and staff, the USU Card Office is managed by Jana Gittins, with one full-time employee and two part-time student employees.

The USU Card program was created locally as a joint effort between the Card Office and USU Computer Services. The program provides an all-purpose debit account (with 22 on-campus vendors), three different meal plans, and electronic verification of student status access into athletic and theatrical events, student health services, ASUSU events, student computer labs, campus recreational facilities, and the library.

The program processes approximately 200,000 to 300,000 transactions per month. During the past year the system has also been used to monitor 65 different events and provide summary reports that assist the administration with event evaluations.

Recent additions include a secured Web access for account holders to check balances, add value, view transactions, cancel lost or stolen cards, and add or transfer money to their modem accounts.

Challenges faced by the program include funding, changing technology, and total buy-in from the campus community. Future plans are to facilitate the use of USU's new procurement card for campus purchases and interface with the university's general accounting system. The card technology includes bar code for the State Library System and track 2 high-coercivity magnetic stripe for all other applications.

URL: www.usu.edu/usucard

CHAPTER 3

Business and Education Applications

- Innovative Solutions in Card Uses
- The Evolving Campus Card
- Partnerships
- Merchandising

The National Association of Campus Card Users (NACCU) has been in existence as a nonprofit organization since 1993. One of its many areas of focus has been innovations in campus cards. Every year, at NACCU's annual conference, colleges and universities present innovative campus card applications, and NACCU members vote and present an award in recognition of the most innovative presentation. Below are some examples of innovative uses of campus cards.

Innovative Solutions in Card Uses

Innovations are not necessarily found in cards with a chip. When looking at a campus card system, evaluate whether chip technology makes business sense. If not, you want to have an "upgrade" path. Find out how your vendor will help you move to the chip without great new investment. The following innovations are adaptable for colleges and universities.

E-keys Versus Mechanical Keys and Locks

Campus housing directors and campus police departments know the difficulty of controlling the usage and whereabouts of tens of thousands of keys, and the high cost of re-keying when locks must be changed. Today, e-keys (campus cards) improve student safety. Scott Madden, director of Business Development for TESA Entry Systems, says, "Imagine one key that opens every door, but has a system to control *who, when,* and *where.*"[1] Today, millions of e-locks have already been installed on campuses, just as they have been in hotels and motels. The plastic card can open a dormitory room, building, or laboratory only to students or faculty

who are authorized to be there. Below are some important characteristics of E-keys.
- E-locks can be turned on and off.
- You control *when* it will work.
- You know when it is used. Access is identified.
- Users participate in rekeying a door.
- Rekeying is done without affecting other key holders.
- E-key holders can have different levels of access.
- E-keying enables accurate budget forecasting.
- E-keying does not allow unauthorized duplication.
- E-keying can be either off line (a simple installation) or on line, which provides greater security, but requires system support.

Vending

Many colleges and universities are looking for new and innovative ways to manage vending. The University of Alabama has centralized its card operations. It is phasing out coin-operated machines and implementing on-line vending.

The M-DCCard

Miami-Dade Community College's decision to move into a one-card solution, in 1999 was driven by a commitment on the part of the college leadership to base financial decisions on what would be of the greatest benefit to the student population. As the Request for Proposals was being drafted, the one potential card application that ranked above the rest was banking. Implementing a banking function would improve the disbursement of financial aid monies to students, allow direct deposit of student payroll, and help to resolve a cumbersome book loan procedure. Miami-Dade has six campuses, three centers, and numerous community sites that, combined, enroll over 100,000 students annually.[2]

The Colby Card

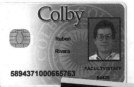

Colby College in Waterville, Maine, has implemented a multitechnology, multiapplication card called the "Colby Card." The card carries the following technologies and applications: proximity core for on-line door access, smart chip for stored value applications (laundry, copies, vending, point of sale) barcode for library use, and the ABA stripe utilizing track 2 for on-line meal plan. You might say this card has everything![3]

Parking

Thus far, little has been said in this book about parking systems using campus cards. Parking with campus cards has been used on many campuses as access control—only letting people park in areas they are entitled to. An innovative, flexible parking system is available that provides different modes of operation that can be selected for the same or different parking areas on campus. The choices are yours to use as your needs dictate. The Auto Fee Park™⁴ is the first product to offer such a wide selection of options.

Charging for the actual time in the facility is a commonly used method to manage parking fees. This is very often done by having an attendant at the facility to review *in time* stamps and *out time* stamps to determine the time and charges. You already know how much you lose because of employee errors. The Auto Fee Park™ offers magnetic stripe time and charges. Records of all transactions are retained, and reports are produced. This system can simplify procedures, reduce staff, and result in greater profits. Permanent debit cards are issued to your regular clients who deposit funds in advance. You get interest on the advance deposits, and there is no cash in your operation to disappear.

The "Audit Trail" system logs each person in and out and keeps a full audit trail of the time and expenses, including the exact date and time and amount charged, making it much more difficult for dishonest employees to beat the system. When you totally remove the cash from the formula (the system is moving the funds from one general ledger to another), you have truly removed the temptation and the capability of money disappearing.

This is a detailed example of how "smart" cards without a chip but with a barcode and magnetic stripe can work effectively with campus systems.

The Evolving Campus Card

The typical campus card in the United States today employs the magnetic stripe, is economical to mass produce, and is already performing all the services discussed in the previous section. As the saying goes, "If it ain't broke, don't fix it." Why consider changing to higher-technology smart cards with embedded integrated circuit chips? Smart cards are more expensive to manufacture and require different readers than those already in place in existing card systems at multiple locations. Transitioning to new cards is a major capital investment.

The cost per card increases with the increased memory and processing capabilities of the card with a chip. Costs range from less than $1.00 each for a magnetic stripe card to approximately $5.00 for a card with a chip. When a college or university can justify this added expenditure through value-added services and fewer personnel, or when the institution can find a sponsor willing to absorb the cost of the smart card for developing multipartner loyalty programs, then more higher education applications will come about. Furthermore, when smart card systems are more commonly used in government, commercial, and banking operations, it will be easier for colleges and universities to adopt this technology. Today, in the United States, few colleges or universities can afford to make the cost commitment to the smart card with a chip nor is it necessary with good technical infrastructures, which is chiefly why the higher technology has not moved onto U.S. campuses as it has in other parts of the world where smart cards are used by government and business.

There are some card applications that will be feasible with the higher-technology card. A few colleges and universities are developing these systems now. Institutions that decide to upgrade to smart cards later may need to make use of transition technologies. As will be discussed in chapter 7, for over 10 years the French government and banking system have used hybrid cards with both a chip and a magnetic stripe in order to allow banks, credit card companies, and others to make a smooth transition to the new technology. The slowness of the U.S. to move into chip technology is perhaps attributable to the differences in infrastructure whereby the United States has more readily available on-line technology.

An example of a transition technology is a smart card utilizing the Epad500-MS (from Gemplus).[5] It can be connected to existing stand-alone point-of-sale (POS) terminals and cash registers. It enables any POS device to accept memory and microprocessor cards, with no changes to your existing payment infrastructure. A battery-backed real-time clock allows precise, up-to-the-minute logging of transactions, for critical E-purse, loyalty, or security programs.

Furthermore, the card with a chip or "smart card," supported by program memory from 128 to 512 Kbytes of Flash Eprom, can perform different applications. This means, for example, the complete up-to-date medical records of students, faculty, or staff can be accessed directly from a hand-held card measuring 3-7/16" x 2-3/16." The added higher level of security provided by smart cards for access control of campus labs, computer centers, and the like is another viable application for such a card. But, the increased cost to set up and run a smart card system continues to raise the point again, "If it ain't broke, don't fix it." Most existing campus cards with magnetic strip and barcodes meet the demands of managing such things as: building access, copier, laundry, vending, pay phones, merchants, food service parking, library use, student identification, printing, ATM, credit, and health care.

Student Health Care

One of the next big applications for campus cards is student health care. While magnetic stripe cards are often used in the United States for authorizing and paying for care, the next step in health care is to store health information on a smart card. In Germany, 80 million health cards have been issued to nationalize the consumption of medical services; in France, 60 million cards have been issued for patient ID and provider verification; in the United Kingdom, over 10 million health cards have been issued for insurance ID and eligibility information. In the United States the Veteran's Administration is issuing millions of health cards to veterans and their dependents for health and payment records. Feasibility studies are underway in six states to look at methods to reduce costs via electronic solutions, such as submitting claims electronically, which could lower overhead by roughly 50 percent.[6] Health care cards have two major applications:

- Patient/provider authentication—whereby the card grants providers access to Internet/Intranet-based database. The patient's card is required to access medical records.
- Medical records storage—to provide demographic information, keep test results, charts, and prescription information on the card itself. The card can also be used for encrypting messages and adding digital signatures to documents.

Therefore, health care record keeping and identification could be added to the growing list of campus card solutions.

To introduce health care cards into a campus system would require a learning curve and transition technologies. Data would be encrypted so the stored data would not be readable without the appropriate authorization, and cards would have to be PIN protected along with a visual ID (photograph).

One of the perennial issues facing campuses today is how to provide greater value to students without a proportional increase in cost to the institution.

Partnerships

One of the perennial issues facing campuses today is how to provide greater value to students without a proportional increase in cost to the institution. Major gains in productivity are hard to find in the labor-intensive business of higher education. Through partnerships with campus card vendors, systems designers, banks, financial institutions, charge cards, Web site support, credit unions, college news wire services, cash and card services, etc., institutions can develop a campus card program that becomes a "win-win" situation. Partnerships between institutions and other businesses add value both to students and to the institution. Partnerships can provide many solutions to launching, financing, and advancing a campus card program. It is important to look carefully and do adequate strategic planning before you leap into a partnership.

Peter Livingston, who provides assistance to colleges and universities seeking partnerships, says, "We help identify win-win ID card partnership solutions that have lower cost, better return, and/or less risk."[7] That is essentially what you want to achieve in a good partnership relationship.

Vendors (e.g., contractors such as dining, vending machine, and laundry providers) can also be partners, as can telecommunication companies, financial institutions, or off-campus merchants. All of these may have something to gain from the partnership and may therefore be a source for financing the implementation of part or all of a card system.

For example, Fred Rogers, vice president, University Strategy and Partnerships, Student Advantage, Inc., applies his knowledge and experience in leading a national student membership program. Student Advantage extends its marketing expertise to promote value to students and their institutions by offering the capabilities and uses of the one-card programs to off-campus merchants.

Noting that many colleges and universities have an interest but few have succeeded at extending their own programs, Rogers says, "Serving students since 1992, and reaching 2 million students and 15,000 merchants, Student Advantage has the ability and experience to extend the campus capability rapidly and successfully."[8] The SA Cash program requires no campus investment and can actually generate incremental revenues for the campus card office, while allowing the campus to retain control of the overall program direction.

Tim Aaron, vice president of iCollege, recommends determining what motivates vendors and what motivates colleges and universities in developing a partnership.[9]

What Motivates Vendors (such as banks, telephone companies, etc.)

New consumer relationships
Relationship building with campus
A "closed" environment
Eagerness to test and use new technologies
Cobranding
Competitive advantage as single or lead vendor

What Motivates Colleges and Universities

Value, convenience, and safety
Strengthening card program
Financial support
Providing card program infrastructure
Providing operating expenses
Management support

When these two forces are combined in a partnership, there are several ways to measure success:

- Customer acceptance (How many signed up? Did they stay?)
- Customer service (How do students get help?)
- Operational impact (Did the institution have to do more or less than anticipated?)
- Revenue streams (Did the revenue show up? This can be assured with a guaranteed minimum of revenue from a partnership.)

Pursuing Partnerships

Suellyn Hull, office manager of the "CatCard" office at the University of Arizona, Tucson, describes how the University of Arizona (UA) has implemented a one card system called the CatCard. This card is a multiapplication card incorporating both magnetic stripe and smart chip technology. She outlines their strategy, the business issues involved in their partnerships, and how they implemented services.[10]

Hull explains, "The first step in pursuing partnerships for a card program is to determine the strategy for the program. Are you looking to increase revenue, enhance the desirability and acceptance of the card, promote the image of the university, provide identification services only, combine many cards into one or a myriad of other choices? The strategy you choose is key to whether your card will be an auxiliary service or an integral part of the infrastructure of services on your campus.

"As an auxiliary service, the card program may be expected to be a self-supporting revenue source. This may result in the focus being less service oriented or innovative than if the card program is considered an integral part of the campus services infrastructure. Choosing to make the card the focus of all identification systems on campus can move the card into the infrastructure as possession of the card will be required to receive any of the services offered on campus.

"UA's original strategy was to look for partnerships that enhanced the services, and therefore the overall desirability of the card. We defined a partnership as any entity, on or off campus, which used our CatCard as an access card.

"When we implemented our program, we were facing a mass carding of the entire campus, taking place over a one-month period. The process required students, faculty, and staff to attend a session where their picture and signature were taken and their new card was produced. While the process for an individual took less than 20 minutes, there were complaints that it was a hassle and unnecessary.

"We used our partnerships with the Student Union meal plan, the library, the banking partner, and telephone long distance services to try to enhance the value of the card and minimize the hassle of actually obtaining the card. Our theme was 'ONE CARD, YOUR CARD, CATCARD.'

"This strategy has adapted over the two years our program has been implemented to being one of providing as many campus services on one card, through one data source, as possible."

Suellen Hull suggests things to consider when developing your partnership strategy:

"Know your campus. There are multitudes of services that are promoted by card vendors that promise huge revenue streams, are said to require little infrastructure for your card office, or are "required" to make a program successful. Be sure to evaluate which of these services is the best fit for your campus. At UA, the long distance calling service was considered by our vendor to be essential to the success of our card. It turned out to be the least used service we have offered to date.

The best way to promote the use of the card to a prospective partner is to determine where it will save them money.

What services give the biggest bang? Look at the overall picture for the service. Will it be well received, provide a revenue source, or reduce costs, and will it work without a great deal of trial and error for the cardholder? Will it enhance the reputation of the card program? If something goes wrong with the service offered on the card, it will be blamed on the card. If the bank's ATM can't read the card because the student is using the wrong PIN number, it will be the card's fault. If a printer cannot read the smart chip, it's the card's fault—the student's paper is submitted late. Yes! Can you believe it? If you have a strong partner who is truly supportive of the card, sees the value, and commits to providing excellent customer service, your program will be seen as a valuable addition to campus services, even with small glitches with individual cardholders.

Offer cost savings to another department. The best way to promote the use of the card to a prospective partner is to determine where it will save them money. "Our library smart chip partnership resulted in over $400,000 dollars in nickels, dimes, and quarters that the library didn't have to deal with, saving them money in cash handling fees and staff costs."

Be aware of different business styles of your partners. Not all businesses and certainly not all campus departments do business the way the card program does. This can create friction and misunderstanding when you need cooperation the most. "Our biggest example of this was our banking partnership. Their decision-making process was top down and revenue driven. Our process involved committee decisions and was more customer-service oriented. This made for very difficult negotiations on some issues after the program was implemented. We finally formed a small work team with representatives from both groups, which had the decision-making power for how the program would move forward."

Look for working partners, not silent partners. Be sure you specify the partner's involvement on your campus while you are in contract negotiations. Otherwise, you may find that your card staff is expected to promote and manage the service after the initial implementation.

Define the scope of your card program. You will want to define whether your program will determine how business will be done on your campus. At UA we limited the scope of our program to a liaison function on how the card could be used as a tool. We do not function as a reengineering consultant for the business processes of other departments. We introduce new products or services that the card can provide and let the department decide how to implement that product or service in their environment."

Merchandising

Merchandising means to promote the sale of an item by advertising or display. In the case of campus cards, many institutions carry advertisements on the card, which helps offset production and maintenance costs. This promotion might appear on either the front or back of the printed campus card.[11]

REFERENCES

1. Madden, Scott, "Locking Doors Through Innovation" presentation at National Association of Campus Card Users (NACCU), San Jose, CA, March 11-14, 2000.
2. Lull, Terry, " Multi-Function, Multi-Campus Smart Card: The Miami-Dade Community College Experience," presentation at CardTech/SecurTech, Miami Beach, FL, May 1-4, 2000.
3. Rivera, Ruben, "The Colby College Student ID Card: A Success Study," presentation at National Association of Campus Card Users (NACCU), San Jose, CA, March 11-14, 2000.
4. Brochure: The Auto Fee Park ™ Universal One-card System)
5. Gemplus brochure on Epad500-MS, 2000.
6. Monk, Justin T., "Student Health Care: The Next Generation Campus Card," presentation at National Association of Campus Card Users (NACCU), San Jose, CA, March 11-14, 2000.
7. Livingston, Peter, NACCU *Card-Talk Newsletter,* June-July 1999.
8. Rogers, Fred, vice president, University Strategy and Partnerships, Student Advantage, Inc., personal correspondence, October 2000.
9. Tim Aaron, "Building the Infrastructure to Support Your Card," presentation at National Association of Campus Card Users (NACCU), San Jose, CA, March 11-14, 2000.
10. Hull, Suellyn, Pursuing and Negotiating Partnerships in a Chip Based Campus Card," presentation at CardTech/SecurTech, Miami Beach, FL, May 1-4, 2000.
11. Pietrantoni, Joseph G., "Getting On the Bandwidth," BUSINESS OFFICER magazine, National Association of College and University Business Officers (NACUBO), Washington, DC, January 1999.

CAMPUS CARD PROFILE #3
University of Minnesota "UCard"

The University of Minnesota has four campuses: Twin Cities, Duluth, Morris, and Crookston. Student enrollment for the four campuses was approximately 54,000 in the fall of 1999. Faculty and staff number about 17,000. The UCard Office reports to Auxiliary Services and has six full-time employees: director, operations and marketing managers, assistant operations manager, and accounting specialist. Since its inception in 1995, the UCard Office has issued over 136,000 cards.

The UCard is used to check out library materials and to enter the university's Recreation Center, St. Paul Gym, golf course, secured buildings, and computer labs. The card is also used to qualify for art and athletic ticket discounts, cash checks on campus, and much more. The UCard offers a checking and calling card account through banking and telecommunications partner providers. The card checking account allows for the direct deposit of financial aid credit balances.

The UCard employs an open architecture by using a x.500 directory from Control Data to house all student, staff, and faculty information. The x.500 directory allows for data feeds to other card-related systems. Each type of card application is controlled by a different system. This allows the university to pick the "best of breed" systems for each type of application. For instance, the door access system is provided by Phoenix Systems. Meal plans are based on a CBORD system. Other systems are in place for the recreation center, library, computer labs, and stored value. Each department can purchase the best software that meets its needs and populate its database from the central x.500 directory.

Gopher GOLD™ is the off-line stored value program at the University of Minnesota. Up to $50 can be physically encoded onto the lower magnetic stripe of the UCard, allowing cardholders to make campus purchases at a variety of campus locations. Because the system is off line, the university is able to place card readers in locations where on-line wiring would not be cost-effective. The system for this program is provided by Debitek, which also provides software tools to encode cards and monitor usage.

URL: www.umn.edu/ucard

CHAPTER 4

Planning and Implementation

- Plan, Plan, and Plan
- Writing the RFP
- Gaining Acceptance
- Implementation Timelines

Plan, Plan, and Plan

The better your planning for a campus card system is executed, the better your system will evolve and run. Colby College in Waterville, Maine, has 1,800 student and 750 faculty and staff cards issued. The card office manager and campus controller, Ruben Rivera, spent from September 1997 to March 1999 moving through planned timelines to bring the Colby campus card system to implementation.[1]

Joseph G. Pietrantoni, associate vice president for auxiliary services at Duke University and a pioneer in campus card systems, says "The first question to ask in planning is: "What does it cost to produce a single card and how would this cost affect the expansion of your program? Establishing a card that encourages expanded use is essen-

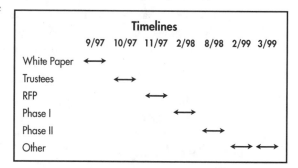

Timelines							
	9/97	10/97	11/97	2/98	8/98	2/99	3/99
White Paper	←→						
Trustees		←→					
RFP			←→				
Phase I				←→			
Phase II					←→		
Other						←→ ←→	

tial to the growth of your card system, and the cost of producing the card is key to how many members of the campus community will participate," says Pietrantoni.[2]

He continues: "A primary element of your strategic plan should be establishment of the card as the identification badge for each and every member of the campus community, including faculty, staff, employees, and students. Your business plan will support the strategic plan by establishing full cost recovery of your card system investment and its cost of operations. Card cost is a huge expense in campus card process, so establishing a card with material costs under $1 is important in system expansion. Low-cost card production opens doors to future applications across your campus."[3]

Operating hours. The next criterion in planning for a successful campus card system is to eventually have your card office open 24 hours a day. Pietrantoni recommends, "Initially this will not be possible due to cost, but it must remain high on your strategic plan priority list." Providing service 24 hours a day will open doors (literally!) to a variety of campus card applications for a diverse selection of institutional departments.

It should be noted that smaller institutions cannot afford to keep the card office 24 hours a day. Therefore, other considerations for after-hour support need to be provided, such as public safety or security office availability, for any necessary emergency aid.

Technology. The next item to be addressed in your strategic plan involves selection of technology to meet your program needs. Begin by asking the following five questions:

1. Do we want to manage and control privatization vendor activity?
2. Do we want customers to review their account balance at the time the transaction occurs?
3. Do we want to ensure that loss of the card does not cause a loss of the remaining funds on the card?
4. Do we want a quick and easy process for deactivating a card?
5. Do we want the card manufacturing and replacement to be low in cost?

If you answer yes to all these questions, as Duke University did, the technology that addresses all of these needs is a high-coercivity on-line magnetic stripe system.

"At Duke, we have a card with both magnetic stripe and proximity technology [barcode]. Chip technology is being reviewed, but as of this date [August 2000] we have yet to justify its need. When we do, it will become the third technology on our card," said Pietrantoni.[4]

This might be a good point to review the various types of cards presently available. Keep in mind, cards may carry one, all, or selected combinations of the following card technologies.

Basic Types of Cards[5]

- Identification card
- Bar-coded card
- Magnetic stripe card
- Dual stripe (large and small stripe or two large stripes which can be either one of low coercivity and one of high coercivity or both high coercivity. The small stripe is generally referred to as the "junk stripe.")

- Card with an integrated circuit chip, also called a "memory card" or a "smart card" This is of two types: 1) contactless cards and 2) synchronous cards
- Biometric card
- Multiapplication or hybrid card (card with combinations of applications above)
- Integrated smart card–cased enterprise security

On-Line or Off-Line System?

In previous chapters, the need for an on-line or off-line system was touched upon. Now that you are in the stage of preparing a RFP, the decision must be made. Once your needs are identified, this will undoubtedly help in your decision-making.

To review: John Beckwith, manager of the OneCard System at Loyola Marymount University, suggests that it is important to differentiate the need between on-line and off-line access control by the number of users and frequency of access.[6]

Other Considerations

Security and proximity (a type of access control) are important considerations in preparing your RFP. You will need to determine:

- Will the card office be convenient for students?
- What sort of card reader maintenance will be needed? How portable are the readers?
- Where will card readers be located, and how easy will it be to deploy them?
- Are there environmental issues?
- What sort of systems integration with magnetic stripe or chip-based systems will be required?
- What state and federal laws and regulations apply? (see chapter 7 and "Reg E")
- What new technology add-ons should be considered?
- Will the Web be used as a tool for administering the card system or giving users access to their accounts?
- How will stored value reconciliation take place?
- What type of system data management is needed?
- Is there any legacy card system in place on campus, which will need to be integrated?

Writing the RFP

The request for proposal (RFP) process offers a rational decision process for evaluation of service options. It helps an institution understand the service offerings available in implementing a campus card system, and it also clarifies for the service providers what the college or university is trying to accomplish. Maurice W. Scherrens, senior vice president of George Mason University, cautions "Remember that for many in the market place, an RFP is their first impression of both your organization and your support services. Pick your words wisely!"[7]

IFB or RFP?

Support services are generally procured either through the issuance of an RFP or an invitation for bids (IFB). The RFP typically will provide more flexibility in choosing a quality contractor. State institutions are often required to provide a written justification before initiating the RFP process, which usually consists of an explanation that competitive sealed bidding is neither practical nor fiscally advantageous to the institution. This review analysis and evaluation, although not mandatory for all institutions, can be advantageous to anyone searching for a best practice.

These guidelines should help you make your choice:[8]

Invitation for bids. An IFB can be used for goods or services that can be clearly and definitively described. The responses from bidders can be matched against the specifications provided. Responsive bids are evaluated primarily on the basis of cost. This type of procurement does not include negotiation with firm(s).

Request for proposals. This is also referred to as a competitive negotiation process. The RFP process provides the flexibility to describe the desired service or product in more general terms and provides the offerors with the opportunity to suggest more creative approaches. Proposals are evaluated upon a set of predetermined criteria and weighted factors. Negotiations are conducted with selected offerors. Offers and counteroffers are a significant part of the process, and cost is often not the primary factor in the selection.

Because factors other than cost generally play a major role, colleges and universities typically use an RFP for support services such as card systems. Scherrens, who has helped George Mason University become a national leader in the field of service outsourcing, says, "With changing technology, we are not always aware of the most advanced range of services the industry can offer at times of rebid. Offerors are therefore encouraged to be creative and are evaluated on flexibility, innovation, problem solving, communication, and commitment to customers," says Scherrens.[8]

Campuses that are not ready to issue an RFP may want to issue a Request for Information (RFI), which allows them to collect initial data from vendors to better plan and prepare.

How to Structure RFPs

The following six stages were identified by Donna Sue Broadstreet, director, Banking Services, Indiana University:[9]

- Staging
- Mailing
- General evaluation
- Detailed evaluation
- Approvals and contracts
- Implementation

Staging should include a summary of the current situation; a summary of the desired outcomes, establishment of project support team and leadership, a review of peer group operations, discussions with vendors and consultants, and establishment of a common vision.

You need to address the following issues:

- Privilege and access control
- Financial transaction capabilities/pricing/revenue/control
- Calling card services/pricing/revenue
- Campus community concerns
- Student/faculty/staff concerns
- Technical support (internal and external)

A sample proposal requirements outline was presented by Tim Aaron at NACCU's 2000 Annual Conference in San Jose, California, March 11, 2000.[10] Keep in mind that all the points covered in this outline may not apply at your institution.

Sample Proposal Requirements Outline

A. *Overview*
    Company description
    System overview
    Suitability of proposed system
B. *Applications*
    Central card database
    Video imaging
    On-line accounts and activities
    Off-line accounts and activities
    Access and security
    Other applications

C. Specifications: ID Cards
　　ID card production system
　　ID card specifications

D. Specifications: System Hardware
　　System host
　　Network capabilities and connectivity
　　Account/activity card reader
　　Access card reader
　　Value transaction system

E. Specifications: System Software
　　System administration
　　Cardholder account management
　　Privilege and plan management
　　Reporting ccapabilities

F. Specifications: Security System
　　Access control system
　　Access control host
　　Access control capabilities
　　Access control reporting
　　Access card reader

G. Customer Service and Technical Support
　　Documentation
　　Training
　　Maintenance and support
　　User group and other client resources

H. Implementation and Installation

I. Costs
　　Initial investment
　　Annual license/maintenance fees
　　Expansion

J. Vendor Appendices
　　Sample system and terminal reports
　　Wiring and other electrical requirements
　　Sample hardware, software, and support maintenance agreement
　　References
　　Evaluation

To evaluate all proposals fairly, the following steps should be followed:[11]

Step 1: Evaluate all proposals for full compliance with RFP instructions and mandatory terms and conditions. An RFP Evaluation Committee will confirm each proposal's compliance with all mandatory items. Only those proposals clearing Step 1 will be give further consideration.

Step 2: This step consists of an operations and technical evaluation by the RFP Evaluation Committee, using a matrix which assigns a point value to each proposal's response to items required in the RFP.

A range of points is assigned for base requirements (base points) if the proposal

Figure 2. RFP Matrix of Base Points

Proposal Evaluation

Step 1   The process of Step 1 is to evaluate proposals for full compliance with RFP instructions and mandatory terms and conditions. The RFP Evaluation Committee will confirm each proposal's compliance with all mandatory items. Only those proposals clearing Step 1 will be given further consideration.

Step 2   Step 2 will consist of an operations and technical evaluation by the RFP Evaluation Committee, using a matrix which assigns a point value to each proposal's response to items required in the RFP. A range of points is assigned for base requirements (Base Points) if the proposal meets the base requirements of this RFP. A range of additional points (Additional Points) is assigned for the evaluation of pertinent factors that are not considered in other sections of the evaluation process.

Step 3   Once all evaluations are averaged, the proposal with the highest point value will be judged to offer the best deal. (Could be Dollars per Points - currently, cost is weighted heavily in Base Points)

Base Points	weight	Company A score	Company A wtd. score	Company B score	Company B wtd. score	Company C score	Company C wtd. score	Company D score	Company D wtd. score
Overview	5%								
Company Description									
System Overview									
Suitability of Proposed System									
Applications	8%								
Central Card Database									
Video Imaging									
Online Accounts and Activities									
Offline Accounts and Activities									
Access and Security									
Other Applications									
ID Cards	8%								
Production System									
Specificiations									
System Hardware	8%								
System Host									
Network Capabilities and Connectivity									
Account/Activity Reader									
Access Card Reader									
Value Transaction System									
Security System	8%								
System Software	8%								
System Admiistration									
Cardholder Account Management									
Privilege and Plan Management									
Reporting Capabilities									
Customer Service and Technical Support	5%								
Documentation									
Training									
Maintenance and Support									
User Group and Other Client Resources									
Implementation and Installation	5%								
Costs	35%								
Initial Investment									
Annual License/Maintenance Fees									
Expansion									
Access									
References	10%								
	100%								

Additional Points									
Understanding the Campus	25%								
Soundness of Approach	30%								
Special Technical Factors	15%								
Operational Factors	30%								
	100%								

meets the base requirements of the RFP. A range of additional points (additional points) is assigned for the evaluation of pertinent factors that are not considered in other sections of the evaluation process.

Step 3: Once all evaluations are averaged, the proposal with the highest point value will be judged to offer the best deal.

Gaining Acceptance

Patty Eldred, director, AFS Auxiliary Services at the University of Vermont (UVM), describes some factors that contributed to the success of the card program at UVM:[12] First, they hired a project coordinator who focused solely on building the program. The result was that the program development moved along faster; planning and implementation was more cohesive; and ultimately, it was cost effective to have one person focusing efforts on the task and coordinating input as needed from others. Then, the project coordinator was hired as card office manager. The coordinator obtained project sponsorship by senior administrative and student affairs officers, who became program champions and were available to resolve contentious issues. Campus committees were formed, composed of real or perceived stakeholders. The committees encouraged campus-wide involvement and ownership of project. Because the UVM card is a one-card program, it affects many units on campus. Committees took this into consideration, and worked with the departments when there were reasons to change existing practices and support was needed to respond to possible new opportunities.

Some Ideal Goals to Gain Acceptance

The UVM card campus committees defined these goals as a means to obtain campus-wide involvement and ownership of the campus card:
- To improve service to students, parents, faculty, and staff
- To consolidate existing multiple cards onto one "all campus card"
- To consolidate photo ID card systems to one centrally located card office
- To improve cash control (vending, laundry, events, dining, library, etc.)
- To increase revenue generation
- To improve building/facility access control
- To save administrative costs
- To be financially self-sufficient

Staffing the card office. It is ideal to hire a project coordinator who can focus solely on planning and building the campus card program. If all goes as planned, the project coordinator should be hired as the card office manager. The location of the card office is very important. Ideally, it is in a central location such as the student center. In budgeting for staff salaries, benefits, etc., you need to determine who pays what. Will other departments who use the campus card, such as the library, student registration, and dining services, share in paying card office salaries?

Implementation Timelines

Timelines need to be established for when you will start and complete the following:[13]

Facility – the design, location, and space renovation of the ID card center.

Card system operations—will you require a central computer, network equipment?

Card operations—how to manage deposits, debit cards, financial records and transactions, campus ticketed events, campus carding, and recarding

Paperwork, forms—you will need the following:

Debit and application forms

Lost card forms including lost card report form

ID card policy and procedures information

Deposit forms and envelopes

Department card and application forms

Individuals on meal plans

New card design and production by card producer/printer (allow 12-plus weeks)

Memorandum of understanding (MOU) and agreements—for users and contractors. MOU to include:

Confirmation of use

Equipment

Cost for equipment and annual maintenance

Card fee

Installation date

Signature lines

Budgets to charge annually

Marketing (see chapter 5)

The Miami-Dade Community College's experience in implementing a multi-function photo ID card has many lessons worth sharing.[14] As the request for proposals was being drafted, other potential card functions, in addition to identification and parking access, were developed. These functions included library circulation; vending; food service; assess to doors, labs, and computers; long distance calling capability; and ATM service. The one potential card function that ranked above the rest, however, was the banking function. Implementing a banking function would improve the disbursement of financial aid monies to students, allow direct deposit of student assistant paychecks, and help to resolve a cumbersome book loan procedure. The college ultimately selected a carding system integrator, a banking partner, and a telecommunications partner who would be capable of implementing a multifunction card system.

Following a lengthy period of contract negotiation, Miami-Dade and the vendor were ready to begin. One of the college's early concerns was that an initial carding of 57,000 students and 6,000 employees would prove overwhelming for an inexperienced staff. The vendor's solution for this was to provide six complete carding systems and a professional team to supervise a series of carding events held at seven locations. The team set up equipment in strategically planned locations and then trained college staff to manage student and staff traffic and to operate 22 physical workstations. As implementation began, the college team and the carding company positioned the marketing staff from the banking and telephone partners in key locations, then opened the doors to start carding. Initial response had been difficult to predict owing to an all-commuter student population who had little previous need for on-campus identification. However, owing to strong marketing support from the College Public Affairs Department and corporate sponsors, 29,238 individuals—nearly half of the college's students and employees—had lined up and received their cards in only 20 days of card production.

Subsequent to these initial carding sessions, Miami-Dade elected to make several strategic adjustments to both the technology and the process. The college had originally planned to outsource the card printing and priming to the vendor, but quickly recognized that in order to achieve the desired level of customer service, it would need to issue cards both immediately and on site. Additionally, heavy traffic on the Internet and the complexity of working in a multicampus environment led the college to localize the chip priming process and to upgrade the main carding server software to a relational database. Staffing the seven separate carding locations called for the development of a formalized training schedule and an in-house help desk service. Finally, the need for consistent practices across the multiple carding sites required the development of standardized written procedures. Once these adjustments had been made, the college felt ready to implement the applications envisioned as the project was being planned.

The immediate features to become available on the card were basic identification, inexpensive long distance service, and ATM access. When the banking partner opens ATMs on each campus, cardholders who elected to open accounts will have access to funds without transaction surcharges. Another immediate priority is using the new card for parking control. Other functions such as cash transactions at the cafeterias, vending machines, copiers, and laser printers in libraries and courtyards will require new agreements with the contractors who will be providing those services as well as much of the card support equipment. The development of the financial aid function will be a major project involving the carding vendor, the banking partner, the bookstore operator, the college's Financial Aid Departments and the creative leadership of the Miami-Dade mainframe programming team. Step-by-step, Miami-Dade Community College is bringing these pieces together and the MDCCARD project is becoming a reality.

Kenneth A. Blye, dean of students at Miami-Dade Community College, says, "Hindsight is always 20/20." To summarize, he offers the college's version of the "Ten Commandments" for ensuring a successful card implementation:

- Secure project endorsement from the most senior level executive management;
- Begin planning with a steering committee that has one or more executive level members;
- Appoint a User Committee composed of interested user and support personnel from all sectors of the institution that will be affected by the project;
- Develop project timelines for all facets of the carding projects and coordinate smart card project milestones with other major technology, business, and facilities projects, contracts, and activities;
- Fund sufficient professional and staff positions to provide good customer service and technical support;
- Assess technical functionality in light of the nature of your institution, and, if you are a medium to large institution, insist on a relational database architecture for carding/imaging services;
- Review your network environment to be sure that all aspects of connectivity and response time are adequate for priming chips;
- Develop a multiyear business plan and budget with sufficient contingency funds (at least 15 percent) to cover any unexpected expenses;
- Make sure that card-related ATM banking services are in place before carding begins;
- Be sure to have other card applications in place, such as parking access that will compel students and employees to participate in carding events.

Note: As of March 1, 2000, all carding offices at Miami-Dade College are open, active, and reporting that they are able to card without incident.

Sample RFP

In the Appendix, a Request for Proposal (RFP) is provided by Oregon State University as a sample RFP for campus card systems. It is to be used for study purposes only, as each RFP must be written for the exclusive needs of the college or university sending out its "Request for Proposal."[15]

REFERENCES

1. Rivera, Ruben, *The Colby College Student ID Card,* presented at the National Association of College and University Business Officers (NACUBO) Professional Development Program, New Orleans, LA, January 6-7, 2000.

2. Pietrantoni, Joseph G., *Getting On the Bandwidth,* BUSINESS OFFICER magazine, Washington, DC, January 1999.

3. Ibid.

4. Ibid.

5. White, Lyn, "Campus Cards Overview," presented at the National Association of College and University Business Officers (NACUBO) Professional Development Program, New Orleans, LA, January 6-7, 2000.

6. Ibid.

7. Beckwith, John, "Planning and Cooperation Are Keys to Offline Locks," Card Talk Newsletter, National Association of Campus Card Users (NACCU), January 2000.

8. Scherrens, Marurice W., *Maximizing Service Provider Relationships,* National Association of College and University Business Officers (NACUBO), Washington, DC, 1999.

9. Broadstreet, Donna Sue, *Writing a Card RFP/RFI.* Indiana University, presented at National Association of College and University Business Officers (NACUBO) Professional Development Program, New Orleans, LA, January 6-7, 2000.

10. Aaron, Timothy S., *"Partnership Formation: Writing the RFP and Evaluating the Responses,* Pre-Conference Workshop, NACCU 2000 Annual Conference, San Jose, CA, March 11, 2000.

11. Ibid.

12. Eldred, Patty, *How to Plan, Open, and Manage a One-Card Office,* presented at National Association of College and University Business Officers (NACUBO) Professional Development Program, New Orleans, LA, January 6-7, 2000.

13. Ibid.

14. Lull, Terry, Fleta Stamen, Jacqueline Zelman, and Kenneth A. Blye, *The Miami-Dade Community College Experience,* presentation for CardTech/SecurTech 2000, Miami Beach, FL, May 4, 2000.

15. Request for Proposal, provided by Oregon State University (dated February 25, 1998) as a sample RFP for campus card systems. It is to be used for study purposes only, as each RFP must be written for the exclusive needs of the college or university sending out its "Request for Proposal." See Apprendix.

CAMPUS CARD PROFILE #4

Loyola Marymount University "OneCard"

The Loyola Marymount University (LMU) OneCard program at its Los Angeles, California, campus has been in place since August of 1997. With current enrollment of approximately 6,000 students and 1,200 faculty and staff, the LMU OneCard Office is staffed by one manager and three full-time employees, supplemented by workstudy students.

The LMU OneCard program was created under the Department of Business Affairs in the Division of the Vice President for Business and Finance. The program provides an all-purpose flexible spending debit account, meal plans, access control (including off-line "hotel" locks), activity control, access to recreation facilities, laundry facilities, network printing, library cards, and off-campus merchants.

The flexible spending account sales have grown from $200,000 in the first year to over $1 million in 1999-2000. Students are able to use these funds for food, bookstore, laundry, stamps, vending machines, as well as off-campus merchants.

Current plans include completing a secured Web access to allow account holders to manage their accounts over the Internet, widespread rollout of OneCard use on copiers, and continued expansion of off-line locks throughout all residential and academic facilities. Challenges faced by the program include funding and control of expansion and management of programs with limited staff. During the summer of 2000, because of an exceptional construction year, OneCard readers doubled from less than 100 to more than 200 readers. The card technology includes magnetic stripe and barcodes.

URL: www.lmu.edu

CHAPTER 5

Marketing

- Who is the Market?
- Internal Marketing
- External Marketing
- Product Life Cycle

Once all your planning and strategizing are completed, marketing the campus card becomes top priority. Much of marketing is about the subliminal (the hidden, not obvious) message. An excellent example of subliminal marketing is Federal Express Corporation and its logo that appears on "FedEx®" packages, trucks, and even their airplanes. Can you find the hidden message?

Very cleverly, and subliminally, you'll find the arrow between the letters "E" and "x." This arrow suggests movement, and that is essentially what FedEx® is all about. In developing the marketing plan for your campus card system, look for ways to market the card both subliminally and in straightforward ways. You will want to be customer-service oriented. Give the customer or consumer what he or she wants, and strive to keep them happy.

Federal Express

Your card office staff should be able to make the visit to the card office as easy and pleasant as possible. Customer service should be first and foremost in their minds.

In fact, the card itself ties in quite nicely with the marketing and public relations of the campus. Design your campus card to reflect the positioning or marketing tone for the campus. Today, many campus cards themselves are often much more vibrant and artistic than campus cards have been in the past. Make your card a physical token that reminds users of the campus. Think of this as the subliminal cachet that will aid in marketing your campus card.

Who Is the Market?

You will need to market the card system to both internal and external markets. The internal market could be considered the various departments of your college or university that will be affected by the card system. In this marketing effort you will be asking people on the business side of your organization to "buy in" to a new system. And you will need to show them how the system helps them to do their jobs better or improves the bottom line for their department.

The external market includes the end users—mostly students. Since campus cards are a part of information technology, you have the advantage of marketing to the teen/young adult mindset what has a strong appreciation of new technology. As a marketing target group, they seek a sense of belonging and acceptance. For example, suggesting the use of the campus card to "phone home" (if the card includes long distance calling) would have a strong appeal.

Peter Zollo, an expert in teen marketing research, says, "Unlike the stereotypical teen being anti-family, teens in fact greatly value family and appreciate home as an anchor in their lives. Despite being so peer-influenced, teens [today] are fairly well grounded. More than 70 percent say they like to do things with their family, and more than 60 percent say religion is one of the most important aspects of their life. In fact, these two traditional attitudes are on the rise among teens."[1] It is important to study and understand your market. Major selling points to students are that campus cards are convenient, time saving, and a cool technology.

Marketing Defined

A widely used definition of marketing is:

All business activities necessary to affect transfers in the ownership of goods and to provide for their physical distribution;

The performance of business activities that direct the flow of goods and services from producer to consumer or user;

All activities involved in the creation of place, time, and possession utilities.

Further, marketing management is the planning, organizing, and controlling of this process. It must adapt the marketing mix (price, product, advertising, etc.) to maximize objectives.[2]

A leading consultant to Fortune 500 companies and an award-winning professor of marketing at Ohio State University, Roger D. Blackwell, talks of "fueling demand chains with knowledge."[3] He describes the demand chain as starting with the mind (of the consumer) to market, creating chains that are based on consumers' needs, wants, problems, and lifestyles.

Therefore, managers of campus card systems need to understand the mindset of their consumers, namely, students, faculty, staff, alumni, and parents. This diverse group of consumers shares certain common needs.

Time and money is on everyone's list. Campus cards can serve both of these important needs. Specifically, some of the most common needs (and uses) of campus cards that save time and money, include:

Library cards with barcodes and magnetic stripe for fast check out and check in;

Meal plan cards for quick entry;

Traditional banking cards to withdraw cash from a bank automated teller machine (ATM) for convenient card access to funds on campus and around town;

You have the advantage of marketing to the teen/ young adult mindset that has a strong appreciation of new technology.

Telephone cards with prepaid calling;

Electronic key for Internet access;

Transportation access for coinless travel/transit;

Small value transaction (SVT) coinless access for copiers, laundry, and vending;

Electronic payment of financial aid;

Automatic processing of tuition payments;

Off-campus merchants—card access to restaurants, pay telephones, and stores;

Wireless personal communication services (PCS) system.

Identifying which needs from this list match the needs of your institution will help in preparing your campus card marketing plan. In gaining acceptance of the card—from the perspective of students, faculty, and campus business —consider the following[4]:

The desire to be in the fast lane of the information superhighway,

Higher education's push to reengineer and rethink its educational and administrative practices,

The availability of powerful new technologies to manage campus card systems.

Certified public accountants (CPAs) Ann and Charles Kelley[5] identified three basic advantages to a campus card system:

• Improved services for the campus community, include increased dormitory security, fewer long lines for students to endure, and the convenience of being able to make small purchases without having exact change. Also, students have the convenience of a card without usurious interest rates and the potential to get in over their heads financially.

• Cost savings for the college or university can be realized by electronically issuing student refunds, processing tuition payments, providing student access to information, and offering card systems for vending, copying, and general cash collection across campus. This latter function may sound rather insignificant, but many institutions have found this to be a very attractive feature because it reduces or eliminates the labor-intensive process of collecting and counting change from dozens to hundreds of vending machines. Institutions also report greatly reduced vandalism to vending machines because they hold little, if any cash.

• Campus cards can generate revenue to help reduce the pressures to increase tuition or reduce academic programs. Long distance calling cards are an easy first step because communication companies are anxious to have the opportunity to make their telephone calling system available to students, and the communications firms are willing to pay handsomely for this privilege.

Managers of campus card systems need to understand the mindset of their consumers, namely, students, faculty, staff, alumni, and parents.

Furthermore, these rates typically are substantially less expensive than the standard calling card rates and, in some instances, may even be less expensive than direct dial rates. Better yet, colleges and universities generally receive a percentage of the charges made by their students as revenue.

Other revenue sources can include the float on student deposits, a percentage of vending sales, and, if implemented, fee income from students using their cards at participating area merchants as well as automated teller machines (ATMs).

Internal Marketing

Before student users will ever see the card, many internal constituencies at your institution must agree to implement the card system. Internal marketing of campus cards should be focused upon the business side of your campus or university. Initially, it entails getting "buy in" for a campus card system from business officers and faculty. Decision makers will want to see your:

Strategic business plan

Financial plan

Financial models

Case studies of institutions comparable to yours

Then, the decision-makers will have questions, and you need to be ready with the answers. Hopefully, this book, and information from related organizations such as the National Association of Campus Card Users (NACCU) and the National Association of College and University Business Officers (NACUBO) will help you through this process. (See other organizations listed in the Appendix of this book.) Contacting the card office manager or director of colleges or universities of comparable size to yours with a campus card system well in place will also be helpful in getting started. Vendors who have implemented campus card systems will also provide valuable information. (See also "Vendor" listing in the Appendix.)

In your preliminary planning you will begin to define the costs of a campus card system. You will make a campus assessment that includes the number of students, faculty, and the immediate needs for a campus card. Then, you will produce a complete business plan, and this is where you will roll up your sleeves and really get to work.[6]

Business plan

As an overview, you will present a "Strategic Business Plan" to the internal decision-makers with the following elements:

Campus assessment

This will include history, technology strategy, stakeholder needs assessment, campus comparables, and projected accomplishments and milestones. Your goal here is to establish communication with the decision-makers.

Strategic vision

Here you will establish a long-term vision for the campus card program, identify who will participate, identify when they will participate, and describe how your plan will proceed as resources permit. Allow plenty of room here for patience and flexibility.

Business requirements

A clear, concise Mission Statement will help you steer your course. You will state your goals and objectives. Describe the implementation phases in as much detail as is necessary. These efforts become the foundation for the request for proposals (RFP). (See Chapter 4 for details regarding writing an RFP.)

Management plan

Now, you are ready to identify your campus card support organization, which will be composed of internal customers (including college or university departments, contractors, merchants). Then, you will define your external customers—the cardholders. They will be chiefly students, but might also include faculty, parents, and alumni. Define roles, responsibilities, policies, and procedures. Other comparable institutions will be of great help here. This is the time to consolidate your information.

Financial plan

A typical campus card financial plan will present a five-year horizon. You will include:

Capital costs (including system, implementation, and expansion costs)
Operations (including card office expense)
Benefits
Net campus value

Vendors and other campus card managers will be helpful in providing data to prepare your financial plan.

Project management

You, or a designated "acting campus card manager/director" will define project methodology, system implementation, marketing and public relations, card office infrastructure, and campus-wide recarding as your system becomes ongoing. Finding the right project manager is key to the project's implementation and continuing success.

External Marketing

Promotion of campus cards to students thus far has stressed convenience and cost savings. However, campus cards represent the leading edge of an integrated information age that extends far beyond the campus walls. Students at an institution that uses a campus card system are at the forefront of participating in a new way of living, accessing information, and interacting with financial and non-financial institutions. This is a tremendous opportunity for business majors, information technology majors, and others to learn a new way of doing business. These are a very valuable set of insights and skills that they can bring with them to their future employers and society.[7]

Information today is characterized by speed, connectivity, and intangibles.[8]

Every aspect of business and the connected organization operates and changes in real time. Everything is becoming electronically connected to everything else: products, people, organizations, countries, everything. Every offer has both tangible and intangible economic value. The intangible is growing faster.

The campus card meets all aspects of these characteristics—speed in processing the card user's information (ID, entry, etc.), connectivity that requires just a card swipe, and the growing intangible value of campus cards as its uses and applications emerge with the changing technology.

External marketing of campus cards has many venues. Consider using some (or all) of the following ideas:

Ads on local cable TV channel

A 5- or 10-minute student orientation video, produced on campus

Flyers and brochures

Internet announcement on campus Web site

Training sessions

Posters and signs

Newspaper articles (on and off campus)

Table tents for dining halls

Campus festival participation with booth, etc.

Convenient on-campus location of the card office

Official press releases

Campus faculty/staff newsletters
Radio (on and off campus)
Local television news

New Markets

When it comes to new markets, college students compose one of the strongest around. Denver-based Memolink began marketing to college students in 1994. By January of last year, the company had reinvented itself as Memolink.com, offering a point-based loyalty-building program marketed to students via the Internet. Through its Web site (www.memolink.com) the company is realizing new potential to eventually tap thousands more students. Today, more than 300,000 members have enrolled free at the company's Web site, and a million members are expected to join by the end of 2000.

A point system gives members credit for specific actions, such as visiting a Web site, enrolling in a partner program, or buying from a partner. Members trade points for gift certificates that the company has selected according to preferences named on member surveys. Among the preferences:

1,000 point trades for a $5-off certificate from a choice of fast-food businesses.

1,800 points saves $10 from barnesandnoble.com, Olive Garden, CDNor, or Domino's Pizza;

4,300 points nets a $25 certificate from Blockbuster, Best Buy, Sharper Image, Bennigan's, or Steak and Ale.

Sprint has partnered with Memolink to offer a calling card that is used for making long distance calls from any landline phone, which is handy for students on the go between school, home, and work. Unlike prepaid phone cards, the calling card program is postpaid. And with the student lifestyle in mind, each Sprint/Memolink customer receives a separate bill, eliminating the hassle of splitting the expenses among roommates.[9]

Product Life Cycle

Marketing 101 fundamentals describe a product life cycle, first with the product's introduction; the product's growth period; its growth to maturity; and finally, the product's decline. So much of a plastic campus card is dependent upon the technology. If the campus card is moving with technology, students will want the card and use it. Historically, most well-managed campus cards systems have grown rapidly, and business is booming.

Introductory stage. In the introductory stage of campus cards, follow these steps to attain your primary marketing goals:

1. Announce the product. Tell what makes the card unique, what the card

will do for the user. Show research findings. Introduce the card in a big way. Student orientation is a golden opportunity to present the card to new students and tell about its uses.

2. Develop initial demand. The campus card is your college or university ID, plus a whole lot more. Create a card that balances tradition with contemporary design elements. Employ the skills of a good graphic artist to match all the elements needed to create an attractive look to your card.

3. Explain technical features. Keep the explanations clear and simple, and emphasize the card's versatility. Make use painless for cardholders.

This introductory stage is repeated every semester when new students, staff, and faculty arrive.

Parents of students are an overlooked market. You can sell parents on the fact that campus cards can give parents some control over where their student's money is being spent (books, food, laundry) while not providing an abundance of cash.

Growth stage. In the growth stage, the card system consumer or user is familiar with the product and understands its features. At this point, more persuasive marketing is employed:

1. Increase demand. Make sure users have the information they need to use all the card's features, including new features as they are introduced.

2. Differentiate the product from the competition. (The "competition" here is using cash versus simply showing your campus card.)

3. Accentuate the product's value.

4. Promote the leading edge image that card technology gives the college or university.

Since many users already are past the introductory stage and have moved into the growth stage, this cycle is an on-going marketing function. This might be done by advertising in the campus newspaper, placing informative articles in the paper, having brochures concerning the value of the campus card available throughout campus such as in the library, the student center, the bookstore, etc. Carding events are big news on campus. Programs that affect downtown business will also be newsworthy for the local community.

Maturity stage. Now, the consumer has used or is knowledgeable of the card. Consumer need or desire is leveling off. Sales continue to grow early on, but they may plateau. Colleges and universities have some control here in card use. For example, most campuses issue the campus card for identification purposes and for access and use in libraries and at campus events, dining, and vending. This keeps the card in use and prevents is plateauing. Nevertheless, it is important to provide reminder marketing:

• Reinforce previous promotional activity.
• Keep the name of a good product before the public.

- Create new reasons to use the card.
- Are off-campus merchants using the card?
- After a campus card has been in campus use for several years, the time has come to bring new uses for the card. Such new applications might include:
  - Single card carrying out multiple applications
  - Cashless transactions
  - Electronic financial processing
  - New revenues generated by prepaid services on card
  - Improving campus security
  - Reducing fraud and associated cash handling problems
  - Banking relationship
  - Secure transfer of funds from parents to students
  - Local merchant loyalty programs to attract and retain customers

Decline stage. The only reason for a campus card to reach the stage of decline would be a disappointing service and a drastic change in technology. That does not mean that any given campus card system could not decline. Campus cards managers must beware of any of these turns of events:

Consumer purchases using the campus card become less and eventually stop. Innovations or shifts in consumer preferences result in absolute decline in use. This stage often coincides with the growth or introduction of a newer technology.

A card manager must always be looking ahead, studying the technology, and asking where the competition is. Most important, the card manager must be aware of customers' needs, which include managing information securely by protecting users' private information; making machines easy to access; making forms faster to fill out and understand; and reducing the number of cards carried. This is an advantage of a "one-card" system.[10]

REFERENCES

1. Zollo, Peter, *Wise Up to Teens: Insights into Marketing and Advertising to Teenagers,* New Strategist Publications, Inc., Ithaca, NY, 1999.
2. Kennedy, John J., *Compact Fact: MARKETING,* Visual Education Association, Springfield, Ohio, 1979.
3. Blackwell, Roger D., *From Mind to Market,* HarperCollins Publishers, Inc., New York, NY, 1997.
4. Kelley, Ann G, and Charles P. Kelley, "Campus Cards on The Information Highway," BUSINESS OFFICER, National Association of College and University Business Officers (NACUBO), January 1995.
5. Ibid.
6. Aaron, Tim, presentation at National Association of College and University Business Officers (NACUBO) Workshop on Campus Cards, "Methods of Financing A Card System, " New Orleans, LA, January 6, 2000
7. Kelley, Ann G, and Charles P. Kelley, "Campus Cards on The Information Highway,"

BUSINESS OFFICER, National Association of College and University Business Officers (NACUBO), January 1995.

8. Skinner, Richard, presentation "College Services in the Age of Learning," National Association of Campus Card Users (NACCU) Annual Conference, San Jose, CA, March 11-14, 2000.

9. Strong, Sara, "Reaching Students With Freebies," Intel-CardNews, July 2000.

10. Bonnett, Kendra, and Dovell Bonnett, "Creating Consumer Demand Building a Marketplace," National Association of Campus Card Users (NACCU) Annual Conference, San Jose, CA, March 11-14, 2000.

CAMPUS CARD PROFILE #5
Colby College at Waterville, Maine

The ColbyCard program at Colby College, Waterville, Maine, has a current enrollment of approximately 1,800 students and 700 faculty and staff. The ColbyCard office currently has one full-time staff member.

The ColbyCard program was created in 1997, in an effort to provide security access to the student residence halls. The security access system is an on-line system utilizing proximity technology. During the ensuing 3 years, additional applications for laundry, vending, point-of-sale (POS), meal plan, copiers, and library were added. The financial applications utilize off-line smart card (chip) technology. The meal plan applicaton is an on-line system using track 2 of the ABA stripe and the library applications uses barcode technology. Additionally, the ColbyCard is used for electronic tracking of student attendance at various lectures. This tracking is done via the proximity technology resident in the card. Also, the security system has been expanded to include the on-line monitoring of fire and sprinkler flow alarms in the residence halls and certain academic and administrative buildings.

The ColbyCard system currently has 23 residence halls on line with security access. The total number of student, faculty, and staff cards in circulation approximates 3,000. There are 107 debit controllers, nine POS devices, five cash-to-card devices, and 1,000 departmental copy cards, as well as 1,000 single-purse visitor cards currently in the off-line financial system.

New applications being evaluated include the addition of color laser printers, a Web revalue process, and off-campus merchants. On a single card the technology includes:

Proximity core, 3 track ABA magnetic stripe (high coercivity), 4K microchip, and bar code.

CHAPTER 6

Security

- Access Control
- Securing E-Commerce
- Physical Security with Campus "One-Card" Systems
- ID and Beyond
- Summary

Cryptography, the art and study of secured information, might not seem to have a need or place in college and university technology. But, in fact, most institutions that are conducting high-level research in such subject areas as engineering, computer technology, biohazards, electronics, and medicine have a need to keep their research confidential until ready for public presentation. In addition, financial transactions—transactions by the Purchasing Office, student bookstore purchases, on-line ticket and reservation purchases, and other types of E-commerce need to be kept secure. Moreover, certain areas on campus are best kept accessible only to authorized personnel.

Campus cards, combined with other security features, can be an important part of controlling access to computer systems and the information stored in them, whether they are academic computer systems or E-commerce networks. In addition, card access control is an ideal component of building security systems. Many campuses are installing "card access" control systems in some or all buildings. Campus police or security departments are usually responsible for actively monitoring and responding to card access and intrusion alerts.

Cards can also be combined with other technologies, specifically biometrics, to establish more trustworthy identification of card users.

Access Control

Needs or demands for campus security come in all forms. Recent hacker break-ins of computer systems at several University of California campuses caused havoc with "dot.com" companies, including eBay, Yahoo, Buy.com, Amazon.com, ZDNet.com, E*Trade, Datek, and Excite. At the University of California at Santa

Barbara, the FBI reported that electronic intruders apparently hacked into a desktop computer in a research lab to plant software that told university computers to flood CNN.com and other companies with traffic that overloaded their systems.[1] With computers at colleges and universities available to a diverse user community—both inside and outside the institutions—problems like these are not going to go away quickly. It has become clear that what we believed to be secure is not.

"Understanding the objectives of likely attackers is the first step toward figuring out what countermeasures are going to be effective," says Bruce Schneier, author of the newly published book, *Secrets and Lies: Digital Security in a Networked World*.[2] "Real hackers look at a system from the outside as an attacker, not from the inside as a system designer," he cautions.

Property may not be theft, as the French anarchist theoretician Pierre-Joseph Proudhon asserted, but property can surely be stolen. Thomas J. Talleur left his 31-year career as a U.S. federal criminal investigator to join KPMG as its managing director of Cyber and Technology Investigations, Forensics, and Litigation Services. The overarching security issues he identifies are immediate threats—loss of communications services (mission capability) and loss of things of value, such as intellectual property. "Computer crimes," he notes, "are symptomatic of a larger overall problem—globalization of networks' impacts." Asserting that "it's going to get worse before it gets better, and vulnerabilities will increase rather than decrease over time," Talleur stresses that "security must be woven into business up front." In determining your level of security, he recommends answering the following questions:[3]

Have you stress-tested your networks to determine their vulnerabilities?

Do you run network intrusion detection systems?

Do you store sensitive data on a network server?

Have you determined your liability?

Paul Kocher, president and chief scientist of Cryptography Research, Inc., in San Francisco, California, suggests there are two basic engineering objectives in setting up a good security system: Minimizing the probability of a security failure and minimizing the consequences of failures. "A good security design goal is to maximize expected security," he adds.[4]

Improving upon security is one reason why the smart card is being introduced on college and university campuses. The smart card's embedded chip is able to store large amounts of information in encrypted form. The data on the card are more self-contained, and only need to be updated and synchronized with a central computer on an occasional basis. Thus, the smart card is less vulnerable to some of the threats facing systems using magnetic stripe cards, where information from many transactions must be sent through networked computer systems. Further, smart cards have more build-in security features, such as secure loading, logical access, E-purse transactions, loyalty transactions, hosting, and certificate authority.[5]

Whether you are using smart cards or one of the other card technologies, security is a concept that must be designed into any system from the beginning, and must be reviewed and upgraded continually in the light of new technology and new threats. Never be complacent. Resolutely opposed to complacency, Talleur says, "Don't believe anyone who tells you they have the answer for high-tech security problems. There isn't one."[6]

Tom Hawk, vice president for Planning and Finance, the Community College of Philadelphia, shared his experience with the integration of CCTV and campus card security.[7] "An electronic key system can be tied to a camera system that is activated at the time that a door is open, creating a video log of the entrant to the facility," explained Hawk. This is an intermediate step to some of the more sophisticated strategies [discussed in this chapter]. On our campus, the video log has proved to be a useful tool in apprehending individuals involved in campus theft."

Securing E-Commerce

Smart Cards for the Apple Platform

A new system that enables use of Apple's Macintosh system with smart cards and as a further security support system has recently been announced. The 2-Tel corporation and its partner INTERSOLVE realized a solution for using smart cards on the Apple platform, based on the PC/SC industrial SmartCard standard. The solution consists of 2-Tel's E-gate 10 (USB) SmartCard terminal and INTERSOLVE's software for Apple's MacOS 8 and OS 9. This was presented at the Apple Expo in September 2000 in Paris, France. This solution offers transparent PC/SC SmartCard and memory card support to the OS 8 and OS 9 platforms. For more details, see http://www.intersolve-tech.com and http://www.2-tel.nl

Windows 2000 Security

Business success today relies on the ability to secure networks to create relationships in "open" environments. Public key infrastructure (PKI) provides a way to manage security needs. PKI lets organizations establish security policies for a variety of network applications and services, such as virtual private networks (VPN) and authentication ("digital signature").

PKI contains resources to manage keys distribution, authentication, and escrowing for an entire organization or institution of users and equipment, and to use associated credentials (certificates paired with private keys). By using Active Director publishing technology and the Microsoft Enterprise Certificate Serve (both included in Windows 2000 Serve Family), a Windows 2000 network (servers and workstations) instantly becomes a PKI.

For further details, see http://www.gemplus.com/windows

Physical Security with Campus "One-Card" Systems

The implementation of a campus one-card identification system should be part of any contemporary campus security program. In the physical world, the highly visible one-card ID identifies the user and his or her access rights to buildings, areas, activities, and services. It is very important for the police or security department to be involved in the design and implementation of the card system. Design considerations such as network security, terminal workstation placements, automated and personnel response requirements, card media selection, campus policy and procedures, and campus data exchange must be coordinated with campus police or security departments.

> **It is very important for the police or security department to be involved in the design and implementation of the card system.**

In the past, access control and alarms systems ran on dedicated private networks. However, a one-card system requires the use of shared network and accesses databases from many campus departments, including security. This integration creates inherent vulnerabilities and requires more diligence to protect the infrastructure and databases from unauthorized users and malicious hackers.

Policies for dealing with lost or stolen cards must be considered carefully. If students are required to pay a replacement fee for lost or stolen cards, they may be reluctant to immediately report such loss to authorities. The campus must, therefore, recognize that there will be a period of time in which the lost or stolen card could be used illegally.

Identity and Beyond

Chuck Baggeroer, director of Corporate Technology at Datacard Group, speaking at CardTech/SecurTech 2000 in Miami,[8] pointed out that everyone is a unique individual with a unique identity. He said, "Your identity is more than a name. It is a summary of what you have accomplished, how others view you. When we all lived in small villages, identity was not a problem. Everyone knew everyone else." Baggeroer went on to relate that, "In today's societies we have the same basic needs for positive confirmation of individuals' identities and permission sets. However, today's global society is greatly more complex than the simple village model. The combination of the ways people interact and the technologies available, for both good and bad, can make such confirmation a complex task."

Therefore, it becomes clear that as requirements for positive identification become more complex, the systems that identify individuals must meet the demands of our changing society. Recent trends in identification include biometrics (the use of unique human traits—such as eye, fingerprint, face—for recognition), public key infrastructure (PKI), and certification authorities (CAs). All these methodologies are being studied, with cards being an integral part of these newer technologies.

Some questions to ponder:

What constitutes a trusted credential?
Will the rapid and available advances in reprographic technology affect our campus security?

Assume the concept of three levels of inspection of identification:

Level 1: the inspector has only minimal training and motivation
Level 2: the inspector is trained and strongly motivated
Level 3: the laboratory inspector is supported by specialized equipment

What advances have been made to prevent alteration to the ID document or the data contained within the ID document?

Biometrics extracts an individual's private, unique information and protects that individual's identity from being stolen or used for fraudulent purposes.[9]

Mike Harvey explains, "Unique biological or physical traits are characteristics that you are born with. Examples of biological biometrics include: infared face and hand vein thermograms, fingerprints, facial recognition, iris scan, retinal scan, ear shape, DNA odor, and hand or finger geometry."

James L. Wayman, Director, National Biometric Test Center, San Jose State University, discussed biometrics: "Science is the systematic acquisition knowledge covering general truths or the operation of general laws. Technology is the application of those truths or laws to do something practical. Just as the acquisition of scientific knowledge is driven by experiment, technology is driven by testing."[10] In his presentation, Wayman discussed recent advances in biometric identification science and technology. He shared the testing and experimental work that is driving those advances.

"Science is done on a timescale of 3 to 5 years, meaning that it takes about that long to conceive of a study, obtain funding, collect and analyze the data, figure out why the results were not what you expected, explain the discrepancies, write it all down cohesively, and get the final paper published," said Wayman.

He continued, "Most of the developmental work in biometric science is currently being done in corporate laboratories. Nevertheless, [we must] consider government-lead programs because (1) Most government-sponsored work in biometrics is openly discussed and published, while most corporate work is proprietary, and is not available for review; (2) There are relatively few government organizations working in this area, but the corporate arena is very volatile and, consequently, hard to track; (3) Past government efforts in biometrics have lead to great advancement in the science; and (4) As these programs are being done with your tax money, this is a good forum for public review."

He discussed advances in individual technologies, and then went on to discuss efforts that cross multiple technologies.

Selected Biometric Technologies

Voice. Wayman suggests, "In my opinion, speaker recognition represents the most scientifically advanced of all biometric technologies. It is perhaps the only technology in which computers can outperform humans. Although the error rates for speaker recognition are not the lowest, the maturity of the effort and the level of sophistication of the scientific tools applied to the problem are the highest across all biometric identification methods. Certainly, the problem is one of the hardest; the recognition of people using one-dimensional data, usually collected in an uncontrolled environment using sensors and transmission lines of uncertain characteristics, is not easy. The speech and speaker recognition community, unlike the rest of biometrics, has their own scientific journal, the Institute of Electrical and Electronic Engineers (IEEE) *Transactions on Speech and Audio Processing,* and a highly regarded annual international technical meeting, the International Conference on Acoustics, Speech and Signal Processing (ICASSP)."

Currently, progress in speaker recognition is being driven strongly by the U.S. National Institute of Standards and Technology (NIST). In June 2000, NIST held its fifth annual Speaker Recognition Workshop to discuss the results of the annual speaker recognition evaluation, which has become the internationally accepted standard for comparing speaker recognition technology. NIST collects a new "corpora" of telephone-based speech every year for this competition using student volunteers who agree to have phone conversations taped from their homes or dorm rooms over a variety of free-ranging topics. The evaluation actually consisted of three different tests:

1. Recognizing a known "target" speaker from a short (up to one minute) sample of speech;

2. Recognizing a known "target" speaker in two-way speech with an unknown second speaker;

3. Identifying the speech segments over time owing to a known "target" speaker in two-way conversation with an unknown speaker.

Fingerprint. Are we moving toward a standardized approach? It is possible that a consensus on features is also emerging in digitized fingerprinting. There are three approaches to fingerprint matching by digital computers:

- Transform
- Correlation
- Minutiae

Transform methods, perhaps based on the two-dimensional FFT or Huough transform, are very popular in academic institutions. However, the commercial organizations have rejected this approach. Given the variation of a single fingerprint from one image to the next, it is hard to believe that "global" transform methods could be refined enough to reliably recognize fingerprints over the wide variety of conditions encountered in the real world.

Correlation methods have been used by a number of vendors. The idea is to "overlay" two fingerprints to see if they match. Because of their variability, you cannot overlay the entire prints, but you can overlay small, selected portions of the prints from areas assessed to be of good quality. Using such overlays, it is possible to even match the pores along the ridges of a high-resolution fingerprint image.

Most vendors use "minutiae-based" systems that identify the ridge endings and "bifurcations" or splits in the prints. The locations of these minutiae and the angle of the ridge at the point of their occurrence are compared to those of other prints to determine a match. It is presumed that two images from the same finger will not be exactly the same, so the comparison algorithms allow for movement and rotation of the finger, stretching between minutiae, and missing minutiae points.

Fingerprints can be matched automatically without digital computers. Every year, one or two companies enter the field to do optical fingerprint matching. Generally, an optical two-dimensional FFT is stored on a user's ID card. When illuminated, that FFT should exactly cancel the negative image of the real-time optical FFT from the user's finger. A simple light detector can make the "match/nonmatch" decision. At present, only working prototypes of such systems exist.

FVC 2000. The Biometric Systems Lab at the University of Bologna, the Pattern Recognition and Image Processing Laboratory of Michigan State University, and the National Biometric Test Center are conducting Fingerprint Verification Competition (FVC) 2000 in Barcelona, Spain, in 2000. The competition will accept fingerprint-matching software from any vendor or institution. The software will be tested in the Biometric Systems Lab at the University of Bologna against four different databases of 880 prints. Cross-comparisons will allow about 85,000 nonindependent impostor comparisons to be made on each database. Results will be published at ICRP 2000. More information is available at http://bias.csr.unibo.it/fvc2000. Regardless of the technical merits, the standards committees may push the industry toward minutiae systems.

University research. West Virginia University (WVU) is proposing to the National Science Foundation a Center for Identification Technology Research (CITeR). WVU has teamed with Marshall, Michigan State, and San Jose State Universities on this project. The CITeR will focus on both biometrics and forensic identification science and will have a strong pedagogical element, training scientists and engineers for work in government and industry. They anticipate support from both government and industry developers and users.

Face. Facial recognition is one of the best of the biometric technologies. No single approach yet dominates. Similar to the situation in fingerprinting, there are global transform, local transform, and feature extraction approaches. A new facial recognition test program is being developed by the Department of Defense (DOD) Co-interdrug Technology Development Program Office, the National Institute of Justice (NIJ), the Defense Advanced Research Projects Agency (DARPA), and the Naval Sea Systems Command (NAVSEA) Crane and Dahlgren divisions.

Iris. Iris recognition is a technology that emerged in the mid-1990s. Although there are a couple of different approaches patented, the commercial marketplace is dominated by the methodology of Professor John Daugman of Cambridge University in Great Britain. The pace and funding of independent tests have not kept up with the development of the technology, so there is very little independent performance data available on iris recognition. Current tests include new algorithms that assess image focus, spurious light reflections, and head tilt. Testing using these current image database algorithms should be completed within the next year.

Summary

Bill Gates in his latest book[11] discusses smart cards as a security solution: "Smart cards, which users can 'swipe' on a PC or at a kiosk, are a solution to identity problems, as with an ATM card for a cash machine. Smart cards, combined with a personal identification number (PIN) or similar password—and in some cases thumbprints or voiceprints—will securely identify users trying to access personal information about benefits, taxes, or payment histories or to initiate a transaction."

REFERENCES

1. Grills, Caroline, "Lead or Bleed: Colleges, Universities, and the E-Universe," BUSINESS OFFICER magazine, National Association of College and University Business Officers (NACUBO), April 2000.
2. Schneier, Bruce, *Secrets and Lies: Digital Security in a Networked World,* John Wiley, New York, NY, 2000.
3. Talleur, Thomas J., "Cyber and Technology Investigations," presentation at National Association of College and University Business Officers (NACUBO) 21st Century Executive Symposium, Washington, DC, February 2000.
4. Kocher, Paul, presentation on "Cryptography Technology," CardTech/SecurTech, Miami Beach, FL, May 2000.

5. *College and University Business Administration, Chapter 15* "Security and Law Enforcement," National Association of College and University Business Officers (NACUBO), Washington, DC, 2000.

6. See Talleur (number 3 above).

7. Tom Hawk, personal correspondence, Community College of Philadelphia, October 2000.

8. Baggeroer, Chuck, presentation on "Identity – Not a Simple Concept Anymore," CardTech/SecurTech, Miami Beach, FL, May 2000.

9. Harvey, Mike, presentation on *"Biometrics 101: An Educational Resource for Universities,"* National Association of Campus Card Users (NACCU) 2000, San Jose, CA, March 11-14, 2000.

10. Wayman, James L., presentation on "Biometrics: The State of the Science" CardTech/SecurTech, Miami Beach, FL, May 2000.

11. Gates, Bill, *Business @ The Speed of Thought: Using A Digital Nervous System,* Warner Books, Inc., New York, NY, 1999.

CAMPUS CARD PROFILE #6
University of Arizona, Tucson, CatCard Program

The CatCard program at the University of Arizona has been in place since March 1998, when the entire campus was recarded. Current enrollment is 35,000 students with 12,000 faculty and staff. In addition, the university provides cards for visiting scholars and other affiliates. To date, over 80,000 cards have been issued.

Suellyn Hull manages the CatCard Program, with six full-time staff and three part-time students. Magnetic stripe and chip technologies are employed. The magnetic stripe is used for meal plans, keyless access, electronic status, and identification. The smart chip is used for small-dollar payments in the bookstore, parking garages, and at unattended locations such as vending and laundry machines. Campus libraries accept only the chip for payment for copying, printing, and microfiche services.

The CatCard program is responsible for all processing and payment associated with the smart chip. Currently, there are 10 smart chip vendors, all of whom accept the smart chip on campus only. Over $1 million in transactions have been handled using the chip.

The card office has developed an electronic status and datamart for use by departments needing to verify a cardholder's status for discounts, purchases, and access to building and laboratories. These programs are updated nightly by feeds from personnel and student records systems.

The card office has recently begun using the chip in conjunction with Sun Ray computer equipment for activating desktop sessions. Plans include expanding the use of the chip for authentication and resource tracking, using the programs developed on campus and the Smart Status and Campus Resource Suite provided by card partner, CyberMark. Plans are also underway to expand keyless access to all dormitories and most major buildings, allowing immediate access or refusal on a 24/7 basis.

The CatCard program challenges include a campus with a very high concern for personal information security, competing technologies for authentication, finding a new banking partner, and relocation of the CatCard offices.

URL: www.catcard.arizona.edu

CHAPTER 7

Sorting Out Cards, Politics, and Compliance

- Smart and Not-As-Smart Cards
- Politics
- Compliance and "Reg. E"

Smart and Not-As-Smart Cards

Sometimes "smart cards" refers to cards with a chip, and sometimes it refers to cards that do not have a chip but have stripes, or multiple stripes, and perhaps barcodes. To keep up with what's smart and what's not, the author respectfully suggests the following method of differentiating cards:

Smart cards

A smart chip card, by definition, is a card with an embedded microchip. This term is used by the U.S. government and manufacturers of card software and hardware. The microchip can be a memory-only chip or a microprocessor chip containing memory and a central processing unit (CPU). Memory-only cards depend on the readers they are inserted into for processing. Although both types of cards can have stored value and stored data areas, the microprocessor card can also process the data, since it contains a CPU, random access memory (RAM), and an operating system in read-only memory (ROM). The amount of hard drive equivalent memory varies from a few kilobytes to as much as 128K and growing. A microprocessor card is truly a miniature personal computer (PC) on a card. There are two basic types of smart cards: contact and contactless.

Contact cards. Each type of this card has a one-centimeter-diameter goldplated pad that has eight contacts on it. These contacts are, in turn, wired to the microchip underneath the pad. The card can be read when the card contacts touch the corresponding contacts in the reader.

Contactless cards. Each type of this card contains not only a microprocessor chip, but also a miniature radio transceiver and antenna. Sometimes called "proximity cards," these cards only operate within close proximity to the reader. Instead of inserting the card into the reader, you simply pass the card close to the reader. Contactless cards tend to be more costly than contact cards and are mainly found in transportation applications.

(Nonchip) Magnetic stripe cards. These cards have no processing capability and are limited to less than 100 bytes of memory. The most common use for this type of card in the United States is bank cards. When inserted into a reader, they can interface with off-campus banks to execute financial transactions, including off-line credit and on-line debit transactions. They are less secure than smart cards but, most important from the perspective of tight campus budgets, magnetic stripe cards cost less.

Prepaid cards. This type of card, such as phone cards, carries no individual or personal identity and can be thrown away when its usefulness has expired.

ID cards. These cards are used for identification only. Many colleges and universities initiated card systems with ID cards. Such cards might contain a photograph of the card user, but they have no memory.

Multiple function card. These cards have multiple functions but do not contain a chip. They are typical of most campus cards in the U.S. today, which contain one or more magnetic stripes and perhaps a barcode. These cards might be considered "not-as-smart cards." These cards with a magnetic stripe plus a barcode serve most present needs on most campuses in the U.S.

Hybrid cards. Hybrid cards can be any combination of magnetic stripe, barcode, and contact or contactless integrated chip cards. Hybrid cards are very useful for providing gradual migration to a new system. Since 1982, French banks have used the combination of chip plus magnetic stripe for bank credit cards, allowing the banks to migrate from magnetic stripe cards to smart chip cards. The banks get the advantage of a more secure card while allowing for a reasonable time to upgrade locations from magnetic stripe technology. There are even some hybrid cards that contain a microchip, magnetic stripe, barcode, optical code, picture, and signature panel all in one card.[1]

Acceptance of the smart card or card with a chip enables the real-time management of customer relationships at the point of sale (POS). This is one of its key benefits, and when the need arises on campuses, the technology is in place. As more smart cards are used, segmentation becomes easier, and marketing initiatives and loyalty programs can be increasingly personalized.

Diagram of a Hybrid Smart Card

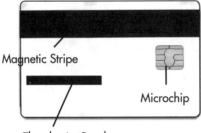

Magnetic Stripe

Microchip

Thumbprint Reader

Politics

Before entering into the world of campus cards, one might believe that politics is not an issue. Not so! First and foremost, most campuses have a resistance to change. This must be a strong consideration when approaching the prospect of introducing campus cards to your college or university. Think in terms of meeting initial resistance and working toward gaining gradual acceptance. It takes time.

Pilot Programs

Before introducing a new technology to your campus cards, such as a magnetic chip, it is important to conduct a pilot program. As recommended by Hull and Johnson of the University of Arizona,[2] "Pilots achieve two objectives: first, they test how well the new smart chip will perform, and how it will be accepted by card users before making a large capital investment; second, pilots provide the opportunity to work out any problems in the business plan before full implementation."

Other Considerations

Once initial resistance is overcome and people (senior management, staff, faculty, and students) begin to see the worth of campus cards, focus on these other considerations:

- Benefits, such as less vandalism or damage to residence halls, vending machines, entry doors, laundry machines, will become obvious.
- Stored value will occur over timewith the expansion of useful data.
- Faculty and staff will appreciate fewer demands on their time and work with card systems.
- Carding will become more streamlined with experience.
- Marketing, through innovative ideas, can tap into other's proven successes.
- Policies and procedures will fall into place as experience is gained.

Your primary goal is to seek sponsorship by senior administrative and student affairs officers so that they will become the program champions and be available to resolve any contentious issues. Establish campus committees—composed of real or perceived stakeholders. Encourage campus-wide involvement and ownership of the campus card program or project.

Consider that a one-card program affects more units on campus than most other programs. Take into consideration the reasons for existing practices and support or respond to possible new opportunities.

Customer Service: A Political Issue

Both Bob Piowonka, director of Student Financial Services and Andy Bland, director of Finance Division Computing Group, at Texas A&M University, agree that keeping control of your campus card is first and foremost in customer service.[3] "Cards must work every time, and that means they must be replaced on demand," they caution. "There has to be a solid foundation for security, and that begins with manufacturing the card. If the office or department making the card does not assume ownership of the security issues, can you really guarantee your customers a secure service?"

They identify campus card customers as students, faculty and staff, colleges and departments, and the university community. "We hold the key to campus services. All we have to do is figure out how to let everyone else know how great we are, and how much they can benefit from our services," said Piowonka and Bland. They want you to be inventive. "Some will come to you, but most won't! Not because they don't like you, but because you haven't yet figured out how you can solve their problems and meet their needs. Create the vision of what you can do for your students and your institution."[4]

How do politics come into the picture? Piowonka and Bland state, "Politics are played when others feel you are invading their domain. That is not what we are about. We are in the business of providing solutions. There are many people at your institution that have a need and they are looking for a solution. Find a way for your card and your office to provide that solution."[5]

Compliance and "Reg. E"

One of the most ticklish or difficult aspects of planning and managing a campus card system is compliance and, in particular, understanding "Reg. E." The time to understand it is clearly when you are in the planning stage, so it will not appear as a litigious item once the card system is in place.

Reg. E came from a 1933-1934 Securities Act, which states that stock cannot be sold without full disclosure. In 1980, the Electronic Funds Transfer Act or EFTA (15 U.S.C.A. & 1601 et seq.) was passed. EFTA requires the Board of Governors of the Federal Reserve System to prescribe regulations to carry out the purposes of the Electronic Fund Transfer Act and to issue model clauses to facilitate compliance with EFTA. Reg. E is the result. (See Part 205, Electronic Fund Transfers of the Code of Federal Regulations, Chapter II, Federal Reserve System, Title 12, Banks and Banking.)

Electronic fund transfer (EFT) services provide the cardholder with the ability to access, spend, or transfer money electronically; such services are part of most campus cards. Reg. E applies to all consumers who use electronic fund transfer services and to all financial institutions that offer EFT. There is no room for interpretation.

Compliance includes initial disclosure when a consumer contracts for services or before the first EFT is made and documentation, which will be further spelled out in this chapter. Other laws may apply as well (such as Part 205.12—the Truth-in-Lending Act, Reg. Z, and 15 U.S.C.A., which cover credit card regulation and credit capacity added to an EFT device). There may also be applicable state laws. A proposed revised rule is now pending that will be decided before the end of 2000.

How Reg. E Protects Consumers

Protection for the consumer comes in four ways:
• Disclosure of terms of electronic fund transfers (EFTS)
• Restrictions on issuance of cards
• Procedures for settling disputes
• Limits on consumer liability

Disclosure

Disclosure requirements include spelling out the terms of electronic fund transfers in clear, understandable, written terms. This may be combined with other requirements, and may be combined for multiple accounts.

The hiring of a lawyer to determine that your proposed card program is in full compliance of all state and federal regulations is strongly recommended.

Details of Reg. E

The full text of Regulation E was published in *The Federal Register,* Volume 61, No. 86, Thursday, May 2, 1996, under "Rules and Regulations," and may be found at http://www.access.gpo.gov/nara/cfr/cfr-retrieve.html/#page1

At NACUBO's Professional Development Workshop last January 2000, Steven D. Shattuck, partner in the law firm of Piper, Marbury, Rudnick & Wolf, presented an outline of the very detailed Regulation E, which can be found in the Appendix.[6]

Also see "Interim rule with request for comments" in *Federal Register,* Volume 63, No. 57, Wednesday, March 25, 1998. Rules and Regulations, Federal Reserve System, 12 CFR Part 205 [Regulation E, Docket No. R-1002, Electronic Fund Transfers].

See also "Final rule; technical amendments" in *Federal Register,* Volume 63, No. 188, Tuesday, September 29, 1998. Rules and Regulations: Federal Reserve System, 12 CFR Part 205 [Regulation E, Docket No. R-1007, Electronic Fund Transfers].

Ralph McCaughan, associate university counsel, Duke University, likes to use the Latin phrase, "Caveat emptor," or "Let the buyer beware." All persons who either use or offer electronic fund transfer services (i.e., users and financial institutions) need to be fully informed of Reg.E.[7]

REFERENCES

1. Urquhart, Bruce, "Demystifying Smart Cards," CARD TALK newsletter, National Association of Campus Card Users, May 2000.

2. Hull, Suellyn, and Jean Johnson, presentation on "University Applications," CardTech/SecurTech 2000, Miami Beach, FL, May 1-4, 2000.

3. Piwonka, Bob, and Andy Bland, presentation on "Campus Politics – How to use the System to Grow Your Card Program," National Association of Campus Card Users (NACCU) Annual Conference, San Jose, CA, March 11-14, 2000.

4. Ibid.

5. Ibid.

6. Shattuck, Steven D., presentation on "Regulation E,"at NACUBO's Professional Development workshop on Campus Cards, New Orleans, LA, January 2000.

7. McCaughan, Ralph, presentation on "Reg. E: What Every Campus Card Program Needs Whether You Like It or Not," National Association of Campus Card Users (NACCU) Annual Conference, San Jose, CA, March 11-14, 2000. (See Appendix.)

CAMPUS CARD PROFILE #7
The College of Wooster "C.O.W. Card"

The C.O.W. Card of the College of Wooster, in Ohio, has been in place since 1992. It is the official college identification card carried by approximately 1,800 students and 500 faculty and staff members. In addition, C.O.W. Cards are issued to other members of the college community, including temporary staff, contractors, vendors, and spouses or dependents of faculty and staff members.

The C.O.W. Card is administered by the Office of Keys and Ids through the Office of Residential Life and Housing, with the help of administrative and systems support staff. Joan Hammer manages the Office of Keys and IDs. The office employs four part-time students to assist with customer service.

Prior to the installation of the C.O.W. Card system, students accessed residence halls with metal keys, and the laminated ID card was hand-marked each time a student entered the dining halls. The Director of Residential Life at the time, H. Dwayne Davis, oversaw the installation of the new system. Card key access was installed on the exterior doors of three residence halls, and an access control system was installed the college's two dining halls. The following year, the remaining eight residence halls were equipped with key card readers.

Currently, the C.O.W. Card system includes key card access to three academic buildings, the student center, and computer labs in each residence hall. The system is also used for age verification, check writing privileges, student government election monitoring, and survey distribution. The college has implemented a debit card system that services the campus bookstore, car registration, laundry facilities, student health center, snack bars, vending machines, and a campus coffeehouse.

The debit card system began in the third year of the operation and received over $300,000 in deposits that year. The college expects to approach $1 million in deposits for the 2000-2001 fiscal year. Deposits to student debit accounts can be made in three offices on campus: the bookstore, the treasurer's office, and Keys and IDs. The college is considering future plans to allow students to purchase food from off-campus vendors and create a secure Web site to check balances, review activities, and make deposits.

URL: www.wooster.edu

CHAPTER 8

Toward Standardization

- Steps Toward Standardization
- Existing Standards
- Standards Under Development
- Entities Driving Standards

On campuses and in banking, telecommunications, and commerce, standards are a major shaping force for information technology. Standards play a decisive role in the integration of card-based solutions by ensuring that cards, readers, and applications will be interoperable.

Steps Toward Standardization

Voluntary standards in an industry are developed in methodical stages. Occasionally, one firm's approach to technology will become a "de facto standard" if it is widely adopted by others in the industry. More often, working groups of individuals representing the industry (manufacturers, vendors, major corporations, system integrators, users), associations like the Institute of Electrical and Electronics Engineers (IEEE) and government agencies like the National Institute of Standards and Technology (NIST), serve on a Technical Standards Committee and produce a Working Document (WD)—the first stage in developing an industry standard. The next step is the creation of a Committee Draft (CD), which is shared with the members of the committee, the association(s), and knowledgeable representatives from the industry. Then, a Final Committee Draft (FCD) is produced and is voted upon by the aforementioned representatives and recognized experts in the field.

At this point, a Final Draft Industry Standard (FDIS) is produced and proposed for adoption by industry standards organizations such as the American National Standards Institute (ANSI) and the Organization for International Standardization (ISO). When the work of the committee has been accepted by those organizations, it becomes an industry standard (IS). In addition, for computer-related technologies (including card technology), NIST, working in consultation with industry committees, issues Federal Information Processing Standards (FIPS) for the federal government.

Existing Standards

It is often said, "There are no existing standards in the card industry." In fact, there are many. Below are listed some established standards related to card technology, as well as some standards that are under development. Anyone wishing to pursue further information relating to these standards should contact the listed organization via its address or URL. Some of the files are free to download, to print locally, and to distribute as desired for personal and organizational use; others have a nominal fee. Selected relevant standards are listed as follows.

Federal Information Processing Standards (FIPS) 140-1

See Standard - FIPS 140-1 Security Requirements for Cryptographic Modules, which describes physical security requirements for smart card chips.
http://csrc.nist.gov/cryptval/cmvp.htm

International Organization for Standardization (ISO)

The basic international standards for contact smart cards are in the ISO 7816 series. Parts 1, 2, and 3 cover the basic technology: IS 7816-1, physical characteristics; IS 7816-2, dimension and location of contacts; IS 7816-3, electronic signals and transmission protocol

Contactless cards will be governed by the ISO 14443 standard: ISO/IEC 14443-1: Identification Cards—Contactless integrated circuit(s) cards—Proximity cards—Part 1: physical characteristics, and ISO/IEC 15408: Evaluation Criteria for Information Technology Security
http://www.iso.ch/

EMV (Consortium of Euro, Mastercard, and Visa)

These specifications for use of integrated circuit cards for payment systems are intended to establish technical basis for a stored value system using cards. They are available from Mastercard or Visa.

EMV 3.1.1: Integrated Circuit Specifications for Cards, Terminals, and Applications

EMV 2000: Security and Key Management

http://www.mastercard.com/emv/
http://www.visa.com/nt/suppliers/open/main.html

International Technology Security Evaluation and Criteria (ITSEC)

ITSEC is a United Kingdom standards organization.
ITSEC E6 High (approved smart card firewall for multiapplication security)
www.itsec.gov.uk

National Institute of Standards and Technology/National Security Agency

BioAPI. Version 1.0 of the Biometric Application Programming Interface (BioAPI) specification has just been released. An entire session at CardTech/SecurTech 2000, Miami Beach, Florida, was devoted to examining this recent work. The idea is to ease the burden of the application programmer by creating standard modular access to biometric functions, algorithms, and devices, and by providing support for biometric identification in distributed computing environments. In other words, an application programmer can use one set of programming instructions to apply any biometric device. A biometric consortium is established under the National Institute of Standards and Technology (NIST) and the National Security Agency (NSA).

Contact: Fernando Podio, Podio@biometrics.org

Multiapplication Operation System (MULTOS)

Multiapplication Operation System (MULTOS) is an industry-controlled standard that includes American Express, Testra, Discover/Novus, Amdahl, Europay International, MasterCard Mondex, Keycorp, Hitachi, Motorola, and Infineon Technologies. It is attempting to build an open, high-security, multiapplication operating system for smart cards.

www.MULTOSTechnet.com

Standards Under Development

National Information Assurance Partnership (NIAP)
Smart Card Protection Profile (SCPP), draft version 2.0, was developed by a community of major users of smart cards in cooperation with National Information Assurance Partnership (NIAP) and the NIST. The SCPP expresses the requirements of the payment systems for smart card security focused on the card issuers and end users. It is intended to specify a secure smart card "platform," from hardware up through the operating software level, on which multiple applications may be placed. NIST plans to publish a NIST standard recommendation when evaluated.

http://csrc.nist.gov/cc/pp/pplist.htm#SCSUG-PP

Common Criteria (CC): Launching the International Standard

The Common Criteria (CC) for Information Technology (IT) Security Evaluation is the new standard for specifying and evaluating the security features of computer products and systems. This includes campus cards. The CC is intended to replace previous security criteria used in North America and Europe with a standard that can be used everywhere in the world. This is now known as International Standard ISO 15408.

Developing the CC has been a five-year international project involving NIST and the National Security Agency (NSA) on behalf of the United States, and security organizations in Canada, France, Germany, the Netherlands, and the United Kingdom. They have worked in close cooperation with the International Organization for Standardization (ISO).

In the United States, the new international standard CC has formed the basis for the National Information Assurance Partnership (NIAP), a joint activity of NIST and NSA to establish an IT product security evaluation program supported by a number of accredited, independent testing laboratories. The main goals of NIAP are to establish cost-effective evaluation of security-capable IT products and to promote the wide availability of tested products to federal agencies and others, thus playing a crucial role in helping to protect the U.S. information infrastructure.

http://csrc.nist.gov/cc/

American National Standards Institute (ANSI) X9.84

Fingerprint Minutiae Standards. A committee has been formed to establish an American National Standards Institute (ANSI) standard for fingerprint minutiae extraction and storage. This committee has the support of the American Association of Motor Vehicle Administrators because of the potential impact on interjurisdictional exchange of fingerprint information. The effort is part of the overall ANSI B10.8 driver license and ID card biometric standard development process. They have been moving very rapidly toward a draft standard for minutiae-based fingerprint verification systems. After the necessary headers, the standard minutiae template will include for each minutia its type, the x and y coordinates in units of pixels, the ridge slope, and a quality measure. This standard is for verification systems only and is not expected to be adequate for identification type applications.

Biometrics. The ANSI X9F committee is preparing to release a draft of the proposed standard for "Biometrics Management and Security for the Financial Services Industry©" (copyright by American Bankers Association). This standard describes "adequate controls and proper procedures for using biometrics as an identification mechanism and/or authentication mechanism for secure remote electronic address or local physical access controls for the financial industry." The current 102-page draft document contains a comprehensive glossary of terms and a tutorial on biometrics for access control, including a review of the available technologies.

ANSI On line http://www.ansi.org/

PC/SC Specifications 1.0

Microsoft has proposed PC/SC Specifications 1.0 for CPU smart cards and readers, which builds upon existing industry smart card standards—ISO7816 and EMV—to allow multiple applications to share smart card devices attached to a system.

http://www.pcscworkgroup.com/

Entities Driving Standards

Many entities have formed standards groups to study and develop new standards. Of particular interest is the Smart Card Security Users Group (SCSUG). Sponsored by the National Information Assurance Partnership (NIAP), the group's mission is: Utilizing the infrastructure provided by the Common Criteria (ISO 15408), the National Certification/Validation Schemes' Mutual Recognition Arrangement to develop and promote the use of standardized security requirements to ensure the device security and data protection needs of the smart card end users are appropriately represented and met in the smart card products implementation of them.

SCSUG members include American Express, Europay, JCB, MasterCard, Mondex, Visa, and NIAP (NIST and NSA). Observers include other CC Project members (Australia, New Zealand, Canada, Germany, United Kingdom)

http://csrc.nist.gov/cc/sc/sclist.htm

Biometrics Technologies and Smart Cards

The NIST, through its Information Technology Laboratory (ITL), is setting up a testing and interoperability laboratory at NIST to measure the performance of biometric devices and smart cards, and to implement interoperability tests of compatible devices and subsystems that comply to industry-developed application programming interfaces (APIs). Participating as a neutral partner, NIST-ITL is cochairing the U.S. Biometric Consortium and co-organizing the consortium-related activities. As a member of its Advisory Council, NIST-ITL is also participating in the projects organized by the Financial Services Technical Consortium (FSTC).

Contact Fernando Podio, fernando.podio@nist.gov

U.S. General Services Administration (GSA)
Federal Technology Service (FTS)
Office of Smart Card Initiatives (OSCI)

The new Smart Card Common Access Identification contract will help federal agencies implement smart card technologies. The contract is for 10 years, with an estimated value of $1.5 billion. Services and products will be available worldwide to all federal agencies. The highlight of the contract is its interoperability for core applications, such as employee identification, physical access, logical access, cryptography, and biometrics. Numerous extended applications and services, including electronic forms, purses, and credentials, are also available under the contract.

http://www.smartcard.gov

CAMPUS CARD PROFILE #8

University of Michigan "Mcard"

The University of Michigan Mcard has been in place since 1995, and there are currently 110,000 active Mcards in circulation. The Mcard is the official University identification card and is carried all students, faculty, and staff members – including the Medical Center and related hospitals. In addition, Mcards are issued to other members of the University community including temporary staff, volunteers, contractors, vendors, and guests.

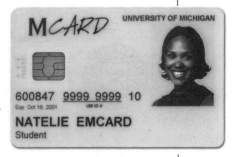

The Mcard is administered by the Office of the Controller and has 4 full time equivalent positions. This includes a full-time service representative in the Mcard Center on central campus as well as administrative and systems support staff. Mcards are issued at five issuing stations on the Ann Arbor campus.

The University of Michigan implemented a universal ID card program in 1994, which consolidated 29 different identification cards into one card that was universally accepted across the campus. This eliminated redundant efforts, provided a single ID for public safety officers to recognize, and increased security through tighter controls over ID card issuance and access to University services and facility.

At the request of students in 1995, financial services were added to the card in the form of a bank debit feature and stored value. The bank debit features links the Mcard to a bank checking account enabling the Mcard to used at ATMs and as a debit card at locations around the world. The stored value feature, which stores a cash value on the computer chip imbedded in the surface of the card, makes it easy and convenient to make coin-based purchases (without the coins!) at copiers, vending machines, and other locations on and off campus. Value is added to the card at load devices by using currency or by making a transfer using a debit card.

It is expected that the next generation of the Mcard will include all of the features in place now as well as authentication for access to information technology resources, loyalty programs for repeat purchases, and acceptance of the stored value for parking, and at copiers across campus. The Mcard is a hybrid card incorporating chip, magnetic stripe, and bar code technologies into one card.

URL: www.mcard.umich.edu

CHAPTER 9

Migration to Multiapplication Platforms

- Health Care Applications
- Bank Relationships and Off-Campus Merchants
- Smart Chips
- Summary

The cost and availability of technology products used for campus card systems depend, to some extent, on the technology that is being used throughout the government and the financial and information industries. It is clear from some of the initiatives that are currently underway that new card technology is coming.

Historically, technology in the United States is driven by government participation. One of the interesting "works in progress" is under the U.S. General Services Administration (GSA) in the Federal Technology Service (FTS), located in the Office of Smart Card Initiatives. This office, as part of the FTS, manages smart card implementation for federal agencies. The office's mission is to implement multiple application smart cards government-wide, promote smart card standardization, build open system configuration, and use commercially available products. The new Smart Card Common Access Identification contract will help federal agencies implement smart card technologies. The contract is for 10 years, with an estimated value of $1.5 billion. Services and products will be available worldwide to all federal agencies. The highlight of the contract is its interoperability for core applications, such as employee identification, physical access, logical access, cryptography, and biometrics. Numerous extended applications and services, including electronic forms, purses, and credentials, are also available under the contract.[1] Among the largest works in progress are entities studying health care applications.

Health Care Applications

Two universities are working on major studies—the University of Illinois at Chicago, under the College of Pharmacy, and the National Biometric Test Center, San Jose State University, San Jose, California.[2]

Piloting a Smart-Card-Based Portable Medical Records and Prescription Ordering System

At the College of Pharmacy, University of Illinois at Chicago, Dr. R. Francis Schlemmer describes the many pharmaceutical-related problems faced nationwide. The problems[3] include:

Medication errors

Adverse drug reactions

Patient compliance

Prescription drug abuse

Fraudulent fills

Drug abuse

Therapeutic failures

System breakdowns

"Pharmacists are often the last line of defense in preventing errors," he said. "In fact," Dr. Schlemmer said, "hospital fatalities from adverse drug events are equivalent to a jumbo jet crashing every day." The *Journal of the American Medical Association* reported in 1991 that "140,000 fatalities [occur] annual[ly] among hospitalized patients with adverse drug events." Further, $46 billion can be saved through cooperative efforts among physicians, pharmacists, nurses, and patients.[4]

In order to turn this major problem around, solutions were identified:

• Universal access to the same data

• Real-time Internet connectivity

• Security for patient confidentiality

In relation to medication errors, President Bill Clinton, in December 7, 1999, said, "This is about far more than dollars or statistics, it's about the toll that such errors take on people's lives and their faith in our healthcare system." The President went on to say, "…a systematic approach to reducing medical errors gives us the best chance for success."

Further, there is a growing shortage of pharmacists to handle the workload in the U.S. Three billion prescriptions are filled yearly, and five billion prescriptions are projected by the year 2005. The number of new pharmacists yearly is not meeting the prescription growth rate, resulting in pharmacist "burnout" and vulnerability to prescription errors. The National Coordinating Council for Medication Error Reporting and Prevention (NCC MERP) lists 129 different potential errors that can occur in the medication use process.[5]

The challenges in dealing with this problem include connecting 600,000 physicians with 182,000 pharmacists to exchange information in real time, with patient-directed security. Integrating two new technologies is solving these challenges—smart cards and the Internet. Smart cards are the key.

Smart Cards Link Everything Together

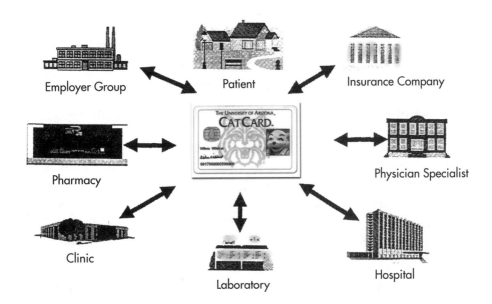

The College of Pharmacy at the University of Illinois at Chicago is designing databases, developing simulations, coordinating pilot projects and conducting outcome evaluations. The system uses portable medical records (smart cards), a card reader, and Internet connection, with healthcare provider access and outcomes analysis. Confidentiality is maintained in the system.

The ultimate goal is to give authorized persons real-time access to patient history and medications—no matter where, no matter when. Basically, smart cards will benefit health care by

Reducing medication errors/deaths;

Increasing compliance to disease state guidelines and protocols;

Improving patient compliance;

Providing clinical database to better understand medication use;

Reducing health care costs;

Linking the patient's database to physicians, providers, payers, pharmacies, and other health professionals.

In summarizing of this database design, Dr. Schlemmer says, "Smart card technology will provide greater information at point of care, and influence physicians and patient behavior relative to drug use, as well as Internet commerce, communication, and education."[6]

Other Health Care Projects

The Western Governors' Association (WGA) is sponsoring the Health Passport Project in three communities in the western U.S. This project is the largest demonstration for state-based, health-related smart cards in the country. More than 25,000 smart cards are being issued to parents. The program was officially launched in Bismark, North Dakota, and Cheyenne, Wyoming, in June 1999. Reno, Nevada, began its program in the fall of 1999. One goal of the project is to determine if smart cards can improve health care for parents and children by having accurate, complete records from doctors and public health programs stored in an easy-to-use, secure smart card. Other goals include reduced health care costs and improved access to preventive health information. The cardholder protects the information on the card through the use of a personal identification number (PIN). Health care providers will also have a card requiring activation by a PIN, which will allow them to view only that information they need to perform their job. Multiple programs and multiple agencies are sharing information under the Health Passport Project.[7]

In September 1999, the U.S. military announced that it would phase out plastic identification cards in favor of a chip-based multiapplication smart card. About 800,000 personnel will carry this new card. The card is expected to interact with their network; medical and other information will be encrypted, but can be unlocked with keys compatible with their evolving public key infrastructure (PKI), which will be carried on the card. Information on the card includes medical and nonmedical data. The medical information includes identification, emergency data, blood type, immunizations, allergies, and registration information. The phased implementation is expected to be complete by 2002.[8]

The Health Insurance Portability and Accountability Act (HIPPA) passed by the U.S. Congress in 1996, is designed to improve payer/provider communications of clinical information and reduce administrative and overhead expenses.[9] Health care providers, payers, and health care clearinghouses are subject to the provisions of HIPPA and will be required to implement the uniform set of electronic data interchange (EDI) standards for the exchange of administrative information such as eligibility and claims. The Department of Health and Human Services estimates that the final ruling on the HIPPA guidelines will be published sometime in 2000. Because security and patient privacy are included in the scope of the act, there has been an increased level of interest in these topics and potential solutions involving cards to address these problems.

Seeking Solutions

At the "Information Technology Ministerial Conference" of the Group of Eight (G-8) nations held in Brussels, Belgium, on February 25 and 26 of 1995, agreement was reached on implementing eleven collaborative projects on global development of social information infrastructures and applications. One of the themes, the "Global Healthcare Application Project," is being promoted by being split into six smaller projects. One of these, Subproject 6, is aimed at international cooperation in developing health data cards and is investigating the relevant technology elements and planning test bed projects. The official title of this subproject is "International Harmonization of Use of Data Cards in Healthcare." A major emphasis is being placed upon developing technical interoperability so that all cards from all participating manufacturers can be read in the different participating countries. Members are Canada, France, Germany, Italy, Japan, Russia, United Kingdom, and the United States.[10]

Details can be found at the following Web sites:

- "G-8 Healthcare Data Card Project," sponsored by the Department of Veterans Affairs, United States at http://www.va.gov/card/
- "International Card Projects including G-7 Health Card and NetLink," sponsored by SESAM-VITALE Project Office in France at http://www.sesam-vitale.fr/Projects/Netlink-G7-En/
- "International Harmonization of the Use of the Data Cards in Healthcare" in Japan at http://www.media.or.jp/proj/g7/english/G7_01E.htm

The next migration to multiapplication platforms in campus cards is banking. With many years of experience in cards, banks have become innovative leaders in applications for campus use.

Bank Relationships and Off-Campus Merchants

The Boston-based Student Advantage Cash™ develops a complete marketing program for campus one-card systems. This form of payment is an incentive for students to use their cards on and off campus. It provides a means to increase levels of depositing and usage. Working with the card program office, Student Advantage Cash™ generates a customized marketing plan for individual colleges and universities, which includes Web sites, orientation mailings, card program brochures, user-friendly deposit forms, promotional events, tabling, and a series of preterm deposit mailing to effectively communicate the benefits on the campus one-card program to students and parents. They can also create and administer weekly e-mail communications with students alerting them of account balances, card promotions, and upcoming campus events where the campus one-card can be used.[11]

Other Bank Applications

Peter Livingston of Stark/Livingston, Inc., in discussing how to "Get the Most, From the Best," suggests setting aside 20 months in preplanning before fully establishing a financial institution partnership.[12]

Get Your Timing Right—20 Months

Implementation (9 months)
Negotiation (2 months)
Selection (2 months)
RFP (2 months)
RFP preparation (3 months)
Preplanning (2 months)

In other words, if your goal for start up is January 2003, you need to begin preplanning April 1, 2001. Then, Livingston says, look at why you want to develop your system and what you want it to do:

Popular 'Whys'

Improve card usefulness (from cardholder's point of view)
Generate revenue
Obtain technology
Obtain additional services (for cardholders)
Protect against legal/regulatory issues
Obtain expertise

Popular 'Whats'

ATM access
POS access
On-campus "spending"
Off-campus merchant involvement
Financial institution services
Financial aid efficiencies

Beyond the "whys" and "whats" are areas of risk, the key campus players, and finally, consideration of possible partners. Livingston says look at your campus goals: efficiency, security, stability, service, attractiveness, and, last but not least, revenue. Look for complementary benefits for all related entities, and with your prospective partner, seek partner goals of:

Profits

Technology

Market share

Market niche

Customer service

And, last, Livingston warns that, "The higher the bidder's projection, the more critically you should study their assumptions. Be sure you understand the role you are expected to play in achieving the assumptions."

Smart Chips

In 1998, Indiana University of Pennsylvania (IUP)[13] had two vendor sponsors on their campus card; one was a local bank. An issue developed over banking customer relations: Long lines at the bank brought student complaints. Efforts were made to resolve the issue. However, the bank made the decision to leave the partnership. Feryal Allen of the campus card system explains, "To partner with a new bank, our choices were:

Issue new cards as necessary

Recard campus using the same magnetic stripe system

Migrate to smart chip technology

Allen said, "Recarding had to occur. The debate simply became, to chip or not to chip. To keep the current mag stripe program meant running smoothly on campus, maintaining current equipment, and low card cost. A move to smart card technology meant:

Strategic vision for the future high potential for implementation off campus

Creating a platform for future applications

Multiple purses

Frequency tracking

Off-line vending transaction history

Opportunity for future growth

With all these positive considerations for a smart card with a chip, the university had other major considerations:

Budget constraints

Gradual implementation

One bank versus multiple banks

Chip size and multiple purses

Card cost

The RFP was awarded to PNC Bank. They offered:
- ATM and debit card
- Expanded ATM services
- Electronic banking on and off campus
- Availability of direct deposit
- Banking via the Internet
- A smart card upgrade option
- Schlumberger as subcontractor

Other program changes included renegotiation of existing contracts for laundry and vending and a laser printing cost recovery system. Campus copying was outsourced. The resolution of whether or not to go to the card with a chip came with the decision to use Schlumberger's OPUS Smart Card Off-line Stored Value Program."

Summary

Therefore, in looking at new health care applications, multibank applications, and the introduction of smart chips to the United States, we can begin to see that the migration to multiapplication platforms is well underway. Will this migration begin to make a major dent in campus cards at U.S. colleges and universities—where resistance to change and financial constraints are a major factor? Will techie-minded students migrate to cards with a chip? Or will the federal government aid and abet in the migration? Only time will tell. In our next and final chapter, let's see what's really in the cards.

REFERENCES

1. News Release, dated 9/21/00, from U.S. General Services Administration. For further information contact GSA's Office of Smart Card Initiatives: http://www.smartcard.gov
2. Maloney, Dan, presentation "Health Smart Cards: Looking Back and Looking Forward," at CardTech/SecurTech 2000, Miami Beach, FL, May 1-4, 2000.
3. Schlemmer, Francis R., presentation "Piloting a Smart Card-Based Portable Medical Records and Prescription Ordering System," at CardTech/SecurTech 2000, Miami Beach, FL, May 1-4, 2000.
4. Ibid.
5. Ibid.
6. Ibid.
7. (See Maloney, number 2 above.)
8. Ibid.
9. Ibid.
10. Ibid.
11. Brochure, "Student Advantage Cash[TM]" 2000.
12. Livingston, Peter, "Business Planning for ID Card/Financial Institution Partnership, Get the Most, From the Best" presentation at National Association of Campus Card Users (NACCU) 7th Annual Conference, San Jose, CA, March 11-14, 2000.
13. Feryal, Allen, presentation on "To Chip or Not To Chip? That is the Question," at CardTech/SecurTech 2000, Miami Beach, FL, May 1-4, 2000.

CAMPUS CARD PROFILE #9
The Penn State University "id+ Card" Program

The Pennsylvania State University card program officially began in June of 1998, and operates at 24 statewide campus locations. There are currently 63,000 assorted smart cards, and another 45,000 nonsmart cards in use on the PSU campuses, totaling over 108,000 PSU id+ Cards in use on all of the campuses in the state system.

The PSU id+ Card office is on the main campus, University Park, located in State College, Pennsylvania. The Penn State id+ Card is the official university identification card and is carried by all students, faculty, and staff members. In addition, the campus one-card is issued to other members of the university community as needed. As a campus identification card, it is used for meal

plans, security access, library, time and attendance, event access, and health services. For banking services, the card may be used as an ATM card, point-of-sale (POS) card, for PIN-based security, and multibank networks. It works in MAC and Plus ATM networks.

When used as "Lion Cash" for stored value, the Penn State id+ Card provides smart card electronic purse, card value centers, laundry, vending, copiers/printing, and POS use— both on and off campus.

As a calling card, the Penn State id+ Card is a cobranded calling card with AT&T; it offers annual membership in the Student Advantage discount card program, combined monthly billing statements for residence hall students, and 24-hour customer service.

The Penn State id+ Card Office is overseen by the Technical Office of Penn State's Auxiliary Services. The id+ card office has four full-time staff positions. This includes a full-time service representative in the card center at University Park, as well as administrative and systems support staff. There are 23 card issuing stations on the PSU campus. Users may also use the card's Web site.

The one-card system was implemented in 1997, at a cost of $500,000 to recard everyone and purchase new hardware and software. There are 34 on- and off-campus merchants who provide a discount to students using the card. The Penn State id+ Card is one smart card with many features, including the chip and a magnetic stripe with three tracks.

URL: www.idcard.psu.edu

CHAPTER 10

Tomorrow's Opportunities

- What's Next
- Smart Card Life Cycle
- Yesterday, Today, and Tomorrow
- Going Global

Card technology is now entering 70 years of growth. Campus card technology has been used in various formats on campuses since the 1960s. Without a doubt, the technology will continue to change. It has been changing since its inception. But whatever the future holds, campus card technology will reflect the needs, feelings, and imaginations of the people who use the cards.

What's Next?

Many areas of card research and development are in progress. From international experience with smart cards (cards with a chip) and U.S. research and development exploring smart cards, the evolution and growth of this technology on campuses are just a matter of time. Today, on U.S. college and university campuses we are seeing smoother, more efficient management of campus cards, mostly with a stripe, multiple stripes, and barcodes. Campus cards *without* a chip have improved:

Dining hall use
Library use
Student affairs
Parking entry and exit
Banking
Student activities
Student elections
Tuition management
Vending machines
Secure access

Therefore, although cards with a chip are an attractive new technology, most colleges and universities have employed cards with a bar code and stripe that perform the above list of applications very well. When requirements for greater need emerge, then campuses will know it's time for a change. In the meantime, study the development of smart cards for a clearer picture of where this new technology is headed.

Smart Card Life Cycle

With technology evolving and the emergence of smart cards on U.S. campuses, even more sophisticated applications will come about. The following figure of a "Smart Card Life Cycle" was developed by the Gemplus Corporation, which has worldwide experience in developing smart card systems.[1]

Smart Card Life Cycle

Manufacturing. A unique serial number is written in the chip during manufacturing.

Initialization. Permanent applications are loaded in the chip.

Personalization. Information related to the specific cardholder is loaded.

Application(s). Application information can be updated, with new applications downloaded and old ones removed.

More Future Applications

Like the Internet, campus smart cards have a direct impact on the five C's, namely:

Commerce
Coordination
Community
Communications
Content

Powerful smart card applications will inpact these five C's, with the ability to check whether students are active; categorize them by college, department, or year; count student voting for campus elections; provide secured financial transactions; allow secure biometric identification; contain complete student medical records; and even utilize a student management system, which, for example, addresses California's reporting requirements, which in turn reduces administrative work.

Some basic chip functions:
• Stored value
• Integrated debit
• Transaction log
• Loyalty
• PIN authorization

Some advanced chip functions:
• Multiple purses
• Off-line meal plan
• Secure network access
• Digital certificates
• Password control
• Banking

American Express "Blue"

In October 1999, American Express announced the rollout of "Blue." This is the company's introduction of a smart charge card with a chip in the United States. In the first pilot test, American Express partnered card members with American Airlines and IBM to test the "Blue" card for airline check-in and boarding. In the second pilot test, IBM and Hilton tested "Blue" for automatic hotel check-in and check-out. The third pilot test involved U.S. West and Intermec Corporation. Employees were issued E-purse "Blue" smart cards to pay for phone calls and small office purchases (such as coffee and lunch). In the fourth and final pilot, Continental Airlines tested selected American Express Corporate members who were issued smart cards for fast airline check-in and boarding. Now "Blue" is available to all qualified applicants. In the first few months of its rollout, new members were presented with a free reader to connect with their PC. The reader is about the size of a computer "mouse," and has a slot to read the data on the "Blue" as they slide the card into the reader. The user can then place orders on the Internet with the assurance that their personal identification information is secure. Bonus points are awarded for repeated use.[2]

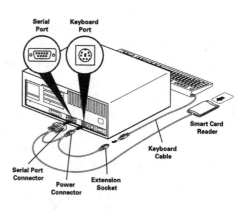

Since then, Visa and Mastercard have followed by announcing the introduction of smart cards in the United States. In Europe, there is an "EVM card," which is a consortium of the Euro, Visa, and Mastercard. Patrick Gauthier, vice president of Visa USA says that, "By the end of 2000, there will be between 32 and 38 million chip cards circulating in the U.S., compared with 19 million at the end of 1999."[3]

Military/Medical Applications

At the May 1-4 CardTech/SecurTech 2000 meeting in Miami Beach, Florida, several speakers focused on how the U.S. military and government medical services are getting into smart cards.

Mary Dixon, Director, Access Card Office, U.S. Department of Defense (DoD) at CardTech/SecurTech announced that, commencing in October 2000, the U.S. General Services Administration (GSA) plans to issue 4 million smart-chip-based ID cards for the Department of Defense. Distribution of these four million cards will go to active duty military, selected reserve/National Guard, DoD civilian employees, and DoD contractors inside the firewall. [A firewall is the use of technology to prevent unauthorized entities from accessing restricted material.][4]

Also at CardTech/SecurTech, Daniel Maloney, director, Emerging Technologies, U.S. Department of Veterans Affairs, reported that in September 1999, the U.S. military announced that it will phase out plastic identification cards in favor of a chip-based multiapplication smart card. About 800,000 personnel will carry this new card. The card is expected to interact with the military's network and carry keys compatible with its evolving public key infrastructure. The phased implementation is expected to be completed by 2002.[5]

The U.S. Army was recently allocated funds by Congress to investigate the use of biometrics for military applications. It is looking ahead to a long-term commitment to biometrics by establishing a biometric data repository and a test and evaluation center.[6]

The Department of Veterans Affairs (VA) has a study underway employing a smart card to evaluate the utility of sharing clinical and administrative data between Veterans Health Administration and the Department of Defense (DOD). Approximately 500,000 veterans will ultimately be involved in the study. The Tripler Federal Medical Facility, located in Honolulu, Hawaii, will serve as the test center. Possible functions and data points for the smart card include visual identification, medical data, E-purse, physical access, electronic keys PKI/digital signature/encryption, biometrics, network sign-on, readiness processing, operations, emergency data, and the DD For 214.[7]

"Bandwidth" Speeding Up the Process

The personal computer provides "virtual" bandwidth or the "illusion" of bandwidth, explained Microsoft's CEO Bill Gates and Intel's CEO Andy Grove. In a joint interview in *Fortune* magazine, the two CEOs defined "bandwidth" as a rate of delivering volumes of bits—the throughput of ones and zeros of software code that are translated by hardware into dazzling moving pictures, vast arrays of data, and communications.[8]

Former Chairman of the Federal Communications Commission, Reed E. Hundt, envisions "bandwidth" as the mechanism that will accelerate all communications.

Hundt said, "Today, broadband (high bandwidth) technology is available as digital subscriber lines (DSL) or high-speed cable modems providing high-speed Internet access and transmission of computer/digital data. Insight Research Corp., a telecommunications market research firm, said that by the end of the year 2000, 2 million U.S. homes will be connected to the Internet via cable modems, and another 1.1 million residential customers will have DSL."[9]

All this activity will also speed up the interface of the smart card with the Internet. Bill Gates writes in his latest book, "With the security aspects of smart cards they stand ready to meet today's E-commerce challenges."[10]

Yesterday, Today, and Tomorrow

Carson Leonard, of the Memorial University of Newfoundland, recalls, "over the past 25 years I have experienced five different student identification cards and was responsible for the process of change leading to the last four. We have "progressed" from paper cards, Polaroid ID3 system, plastic laminated backed, Mylar cards in a plastic pouch, to a smart chip card. Each card was picked for advantages and replaced for its disadvantages. Sometimes changes were made in an effort to use technology to solve existing problems. Other times, technology was used because it was available and then problems were found for it to solve. Were all our decisions correct? Did we make the right choice each and every time? The short answer is 'No.' When decisions are made in our environments and the procedures dictated by the political environment are followed, then the decisions made are often the ones demanded by the system, and no other decision is realistically possible. With changing technologies, individuals, and structures, a decision may be right today and wrong in five years and forgotten in ten."[11]

Going Global

One of the ironies of global card development is the explosion of cards with a chip throughout the world, while only now are card developers in the U.S. catching on to the many ways smart cards can pay for themselves. Jeffrey D. Sachs, professor of International Trade, and Galen L. Stone, Director of the Institute for International Development, both of Harvard University, wrote in the book, *The Ris-*

ing Tide, "To gauge the powerful positive forces that accompany globalization, it is good to start with a clear appreciation of the phenomenon itself. For the first time in history, virtually all of the world's nations have adopted market-based economic policies and open trading systems, thereby linking more than five billion people in global markets for goods, services, capital, and technology." They go on to say, "The results include a stunning growth of world trade; a burgeoning of capital flows to emerging markets; and a rapidly evolving international division of labor, with production and technology being relocated around the globe. The full ramifications of these dramatic changes are only now coming into focus."[12]

In May 2000, *The Washington Post* newspaper reported that, "In just 5 years, the Internet has gone from the strange to the standard. The World Wide Web has gone from a strange new frontier to a powerful medium for sharing information, transacting business, and communicating with people across the room or across the globe."[13] This means that in today's technology, with increased high-speed access to the Internet, the demand for greater security of E-commerce information placed on the Internet will lead to greater use of smart cards to provide that security. This demand will undoubtedly extend to college and university campuses throughout the U.S.

Norris and Olson, in their book, *E-Business in Education,* tie E-commerce with debit, credit, and smart -card options, "Over the next two to three years, the emergence of pervasive electronic commerce applications will transform the manner in which colleges and universities conduct their most basic business functions. This transformation will be signaled by ubiquitous and uniform access to networked computers, collaborative initiatives among institutions and business solution providers, and legislative reform of key regulatory law. The results will include reduced operating expense, enhanced service delivery, the outsourcing (or co-sourcing) of noncore business operations, and a return to a focus on education and research."[14] Campus cards will be used to pay for all on-campus products and services.

IBM, Philips Semiconductors, and Junghans have created an exciting new type of watch, worn exactly like a standard wristwatch, that provides far greater functionality than just time measurement. The Junghans radio-controlled, solar ceramic watch uses an integrated contactless OpenPlatform/JavaCard-enabled smart card controller integrated circuit (IC) to extend functionality into the area of open, multiapplication information technology (IT) use with convenient contactless operation for users. Applications that may be loaded on demand to the watch are electronic tickets, door keys, electronic purses, and ID information.[15] *Star Wars,* look out!

The World Future Society makes a science out of predicting the future. Some of the Society's well-known experts whose ideas have appeared in its journal, *The Futurist,* include Nobel Prize-winning chemist Glenn Seaborg, economist Peter F. Drucker, and new media visionary Nicholas Negroponte. Among the Society's "Ten Innovative Products for the Next Decade" is the "electronic wallet." This is described as a "smart card to replace money, keys, driver's license, medical records, etc."[16]

The fact is that campus cards with a magnetic stripe are already proving capable of performing many of these tasks! Can campus cards with the addition of a memory chip prove able in the next decade to carry innovations to a new, yet-to-be determined scope? Time will tell.

REFERENCES

1. Grills, Caroline, "Get Smart, Get Carded," BUSINESS OFFICER, National Association of College and University Business Officers (NACUBO), Washington, DC, July 2000.
2. Maloney, Daniel L., presentation on "Health Smart Cards: Looking Back and Looking Forward," at CardTech/SecurTech 2000, Miami Beach, FL, May 1-4, 2000. See also American Express "Blue" on Web: www.americanexpress/blue.com
3. Gauthier, Patrick, quoted in "Smart Cards Are Here To Stay," by Nancy Blackburn, Intele-CardNews, May 2000, Quality Publishing, Inc., Houston, TX. See also Web: www.visa.com
4. Dixon, Mary, presentation on "Government Applications," at CardTech/SecurTech 2000, Miami Beach, FL, May 1-4, 2000.
5. Ibid. (See number 2 above.)
6. Wayman, Jim, presentation on "Biometric Technology: New Test/Development Initiatives," at CardTech/SecurTech 2000, Miami Beach, FL, May 1-4, 2000.
7. Lewis, Dennis M., presentation on "Health Care Applications," at CardTech/SecurTech 2000, Miami Beach, FL, May 1-4, 2000.
8. Gates, Bill, *Business @ The Speed of Thought: Using A Digital Nervous System,* Warner Books, Inc., New York, NY, 1999.
9. Hundt, Reed E., *You Say You Want A Revolution,* Yale University Press, New Haven, CT, 2000.
10. Ibid. (See number 8 above.)
11. Leonard, Carson, *"From Paper to Smart Chip" 25 Years of Campus Cards,"* CARD TALK, National Association of Campus Card Users (NACCU), June-July 1999.
12. *The Rising Tide,* Edited by Jerry J. Jasinowski, John Wiley & Sons, Inc., New York, NY, 1998.
13. *The Washington Post,* "A Dot-Com World," May 17, 2000.
14. Norris, Donald M. and Mark A. Olson, *E-Business in Education: Building Competencies for Tomorrow's Opportunities,* National Association of College and University Business Officers, Washington, DC, 1999.
15. News Release from Philips Semiconductors, dated October 2,000.
16. *Special Report,* published by the World Future Society, Bethesda, MD, Fall 2000.

CAMPUS CARD PROFILE #10
Duke University "The DukeCard"

The Duke University DukeCard program has been in place since 1985, and there are over 55,000 active DukeCards currently in circulation. The DukeCard system is the largest on-line card system in the nation, with a network of over 900 card readers that process more than 300,000 transactions each day.

BLUE DEVIL, DUKE
AUXILIARY SERVICES

The DukeCard is the official identification card for all university, Medical Center, and Health System students, faculty, and staff members. It allows cardholders to make purchases, enter facilities, check out library books, and perform many other functions. In addition, DukeCards are issued to other members of the university community including temporary staff, volunteers, contractors, vendors, alumni, and conference participants.

The DukeCard program is administered by the DukeCard Office, and was the first program in the nation to operate its card office 24 hours a day, 7 days a week. The department has 13 full-time equivalent positions, and offers customer support from its main office on Duke University's West Campus and from its satellite office located in the Duke University Medical Center.

When the DukeCard was implemented in 1985, the it immediately consolidated four different identification cards into a single card that was universally accepted across the campus. This eliminated redundant efforts, provided a single ID for public safety officers to recognize, and increased security through tighter controls over ID card issuance and access to university services and faculty.

For 15 years, the DukeCard Office has provided the Duke University community with efficient, accurate, and secure solutions for a vast number of applications while maintaining the highest standards of customer service for the entire Duke community. The DukeCard system has become an exemplary model for other colleges and universities to study. The present technology employed on the DukeCard is one magnetic stripe and a barcode.

URL: www.dukecard.duke.edu

APPENDIX

ACRONYMS

Newcomers to the card tech industry will find themselves drowning in acronyms. Therefore, in consideration of these new people, here is an A-Z list of some commonly bantered about acronyms. Further, for the newcomer, throughout this book you will find the words spelled out when they first appear in a chapter, followed by the acronym, for example: information technology (IT). Hereinafter, the acronym will be used after the introduction of the word in a chapter.

ABA	American Banking Association
ACH	Automated Clearing House
AIM	Alternative Investment Market
APDU	(commands between the card and the terminal)
API	Application Programming Interface
ASR	answer seizure ratio
ATM	automated teller machine
B2B	business-to-business
BEM	back-end modules
BT	British Telecom
EMV	Europay/MasterCard/Visa (host environment for financial applications)
C2C	cash-to-card
CA	Certificate Authority
CAPI	(Microsoft-specific API, used in cryptography)
CAT	computer-aided transcript
CEPS	Common Electronic Purse Specifications
CIA	Controlled Internet Access
CIC	Carrier Identification Code
CIP	Cryptographic Interface Provider

CLI	call line identification
CMYB	Cyan, Magenta, Yellow, and Black. Card print production colors created using inks based in cyan (blue), magenta (pink) yellow, and black. The four printing process colors. (See also PMS.)
COM	Component Object Model
CP	Communication Profile
CPP	calling party pays
CPU	Central Processing Unit
C-SET	Chip-secured electronic transaction
CTIA	Cellular Telecommunications Industry Association
DDA	demand deposit account
DFA	Differential Form Analysis
DPA	Differential Power Analysis
DRP	disaster recovery plan
DSL	Digital Subscriber Line
E2E	End-to-End
ECCSA	European Calling Card Services Association
EDI	Electronic Data Interchange
EDT	electronic data transfer
EES	End-to-end security/solutions

EFT	electronic fund transfer
EFTA	Electronic Fund Transfer Act
EP	Electronic purse
ERP	Enterprise Resource Planning
FCC	Federal Communications Commission
FET	federal excise tax
FoIP	Fax over Internet Protocol
GIP	Genie Internet Portal
GPRS	general packet radio system
GSM	(run authentication)
GUI	graphical user interface
HID	(type of proximity reader)
HSCSD	high speed circuit switched data
HTML	HyperText Markup Language
IAC	International Agent Channel
IBT	international business traveler
IC	integrated circuit(s)
ICT	incident command team
IDT	(a type of prepaid calling card)
IEC	Integral Encryption Circuits
IP	Internet Protocol
IRS	Internal Revenue Service
IS	Internet Server
ISO	International Standards Organization
IT	information technology
ITA	International Telecard Association
ITFS	International toll-free based services
LCR	least cost routing
LEC	local exchange carrier
LOC	Local Services
MOU	memorandum of understanding
NACCU	National Association of Campus Card Users
NACUBO	National Association of College and University Business Officers
OCF	open card framework (non-Windows devices, appliances)
OLT	On-line transactions
OPR	Operator Services
OS	operating system
OSS	Open System Solution

OTA	Over-the-air
OTM	on the move market
OVI	(type of ink for cards)
PC	personal computer
PCR	portable card readers
PDD	post dialing delay
PIN	personal identification number
PKCS	(used in cryptography)
PKI	Public Key Infrastructures
PLA	(memory cards wired logic—pre-paid cards)
PLC	product life cycle
PMS	Pantone Matching System – the industry standard in mixing ink colors for exact match for cards.
POS	point-of-sale
POSA	point-of-sale-activation
PRS	premium rate services
PSTN	(a type of phone circuit access)
PTC	prepaid telephone card
PVC	polyvinyl chloride, a thin thermoplastic resin used for cards
RAM	Random Access Memory
RFP	request for proposal
ROM	Remote Operator Services
SC	smart card
SCSI	(type of interface)
SCEG	Smart Card Expert Group
SD	secure digital card
SET	secure electronic transaction
SMS	short message service
S/N Ratio	signal-to-noise ratio
SP	service provider
SPA	service provider application
SPF	Single Point File
SPS	Single Point Security
SS	Security Servers
SSL	secure sockets layer
SSN	Social Security number
SV	Stored Value
TCI	Telecommunications Composite Index
TCO	Total Cost of Ownership

TDM	(a type of network)
TGA	Trusted Global Advisor
TP	technology providers
TSI	Telecommunications Sectors Index
TSP	Telephony Services Platform
UPC	universal product code
USB	universal serial bus
UV	ultraviolet (ink embedded in cards for security)
VAR	Value-added reseller
VAS	value-added service
VMS	Vending Management System
VoD	voice over data
VoIP	voice over Internet protocol
VPN	Virtual Private Networks
WAP	wireless application protocol
WEB	acronym for World Wide Web (also WWW)
WIA	Wireless Information Age
WIM	WAP Identity Module
WSG	Wireless Security Group

ORGANIZATIONS

**ASSOCIATION OF COLLEGE &
UNIVERSITY TELECOMMUNICATION
ADMINISTRATORS (ACUTA)**
152 W. Zandale, Suite 200
Lexington, KY 40503
Tel: (859) 278-3338; Fax: (859) 278-3268
Web: www.acuta.org

CARDTECH/SECURTECH
Annual conference
7200 Wisconsin Ave., Ste. 308
Bethesda, MD 20814
Contact: Ben Miller, Chairman
Tel: (301) 654-0551; Fax: (301) 654-0287
E-mail: ctst@crst.com

**COMMUNICATIONS FRAUD
CONTROL ASSOCIATION
CONFERENCE**
3030 N. Central Ave., Suite 804
Phoenix, AZ 85012
Tel: (602) 265-2322; Fax: (602) 265-1015
E-mail: fraud@cfa.org
Web: www.cfca.org

**INTERNATIONAL CARD MANUFACTUR-
ERS ASSOCIATION (ICMA)**
191 Clarksville Road
Princeton Junction, NJ 08550
Tel: (609) 799-4900; Fax: (609) 799-7032
E-mail: comments@icma.com
Web: www.icma.com

**INTERNATIONAL TELECARD
ASSOCIATION (ITA)**
904 Massachusetts Ave., N.E.
Washington, DC 20002
Tel: (202) 544-4448; Fax: (202) 547-7417
E-mail: inquires@telecard.com
Web: www.telecard.org

**NATIONAL ASSOCIATION OF
CAMPUS CARD USERS (NACCU)**
518 South Three Notch Street
Troy, AL 36081
Tel: (334) 808-4258; Fax: (334) 808-4260
E-mail: execdir@naccu.org
Web: www.naccu.org

**NATIONAL ASSOCIATION OF
COLLEGE AUXILIARY SERVICES**
7 Boar's Head Lane
Charlottesville, VA 22903
Tel: (804) 245-8425; Fax: (804) 245-8453
Web: www.nacas.org

**NATIONAL ASSOCIATION OF
COLLEGE AND UNIVERSITY
BUSINESS OFFICERS (NACUBO)**
2501 M Street, NW, Suite 400
Washington, DC 20037-1308
Tel: (202) 861-2500; Fax: (202) 296-1592
Web: www.nacubo.org

**NATIONAL ASSOCIATION OF COLLEGE
AND UNIVERSITY FOOD SERVICES
(NACUFS)**
1405 S. Harrison Rd., Suite 305
Manly Miles Bldg., Michigan State University
East Lansing, MI 48842-5242
Contact: Dr. Joseph H. Spina, CAE
Executive Director
Tel: (517) 332-2494; Fax: (517) 332-8144
E-mail: jhspina@pilot.msu.edu
Web: www.nacufs.org

SMART CARD INDUSTRY ASSOCIATION
191 Clarksville Road
Lawrenceville, NJ 08648
Contact: Lynn M. Russo, Association Manager
Tel: 609-799-5654; Fax: 609-799-7032
E-mail: lrusso@scia.org

**TELECOMMUNICATION RESELLERS
ASSOCIATION (TRA)**
1401 K St., N.W. Suite 600
Washington, D.C. 20005
Tel: (202) 835-9898; Fax: (202) 835-9893
Web: www.tra.org

OUTLINE OF SELECTED REGULATION E PROVISIONS

At NACUBO's Professional Development Workshop last January 2000, Steven D. Shattuck, partner in the law firm of Piper, Marbury, Rudnick & Wolf, presented an outline of the very detailed Regulation E which is provided as follows.

Outline of Selected
Regulation E Provisions

Table of Contents

OUTLINE OF SELECTED REGULATION E PROVISIONS

Introduction

This outline summarizes certain provisions of Regulation E, as it relates to debit cards issued by educational institutions. Regulation E (or Reg. E or the Regulation) is a regulation issued by the Federal Reserve Board which implements the federal Electronic Fund Transfers Act. Reg. E has the force of law, and a violation of Reg. E carries with it the applicable statutory penalties.

For the purpose of explaining the requirements of the Regulation, this presentation assumes that Reg. E applies to debit cards issued by educational institutions. However, the application of the Regulation to these debit card programs, in whole or in part, is open to question, because at least some features of these programs were not in existence when Congress passed the Act in the late 1970s. These issues have not been addressed in any reported legal decisions that the author is aware of. Despite the practical difficulties of compliance, and despite the ambiguity of the Regulation in some cases, any issuer of debit cards should review the Regulation carefully, with its counsel, and make an informed judgment about compliance.

In the outline, the author has not tried to distinguish between exact quotations and summaries of the Regulation, although editorial comments are usually included within parenthesis. *The Regulation itself should always be consulted when any specific point is at issue.*

I. Application of Regulation E

A. **Key Definitions.** The defined terms in Section 205.2 establish whether Reg. E applies to debit cards issued by educational institutions.

1. *Access Device* means a card, code or other means of access to a consumer's *account* that may be used for the purpose of initiating *electronic fund transfers.* §205.2(a).

2. *Account* means a consumer asset account held directly or indirectly by a *financial institution* and established primarily for personal, family or household purposes. 205.2(b). [This is probably the most significant definition relating to the scope of Reg. E.]

3. *Electronic Fund Transfer* means any transfer of funds initiated through an *electronic terminal* for the purpose of authorizing a *financial institution* to debit or credit an *account.* The term includes point of sale transfers. It includes all transfers resulting from debit card transactions, including those that do not involve an electronic terminal at the time of the transaction. §205.3(b).

4. *Electronic Terminal* means an electronic device through which a consumer may initiate an electronic fund transfer. The term includes point of sale terminals, as well as ATM's and cash dispensing machines. §205.2(h).

C

5. *Financial Institution* means any person who, directly or indirectly, holds an *account* belonging to a consumer. The term also includes any person who issues an *access device* and agrees with a consumer to provide electronic fund transfer services. §205.2(i). *[Therefore, despite the misleading term, a "financial institution" can mean any ordinary business entity which satisfies this definition, and is clearly not limited to banks, credit unions, etc.]*

B. **Other Definitions.**   There are other important definitions in §205.2 which relate to other matters covered in this outline, such as *"unauthorized electronic fund transfer,"* (§205.2(m)) and *"business day."* (§2.05.2(d)).

C. **Conclusion Regarding Applicability.**   Based on a strict reading of the above definitions, and putting aside whether Congress intended for the Act to cover colleges as well as banks, Reg. E seems to apply to a college which holds, directly or indirectly, a sum of money for a student, and issues an access device to that student for use at campus or off-campus point of sale terminals. However, in a situation in which the consumer has paid a sum of money and no longer has control over it, the application of the Regulation is much more questionable.

II.   Issuance of Access Devices (§205.5)

A. **General Rule.**   In general, an institution may issue an access device to a consumer only in response to an oral or written request or application for the device, or as a renewal of or in substitution for an accepted access device.

B. **Exceptions.**

1. An exception to the general rule is that an access device can be distributed to the consumer on an unsolicited basis:

    (a)   *if* it is not validated [and therefore cannot be used],

    (b)   *if* the initial disclosures required by §205.7 are given at the time of the distribution [These disclosures are more fully discussed in part IV];

    (c)   *if* the distribution is accompanied by a clear explanation that the access device is not validated and how the consumer may dispose of the access device if validation is not desired [there is a model form in the Appendix to Reg. E for this disclosure]; and

    (d)   *if* the access device is validated only in response to the consumer's oral or written request or application for validation *and* after verification of the consumer's identity.

2. As noted in exception (a) above, an institution may issue an unsolicited debit card and a personal identification number (PIN) to a consumer, as long as the institution's system is programmed not to accept the consumer's card and PIN

until the consumer has requested validation. The institution must verify the consumer's identity by some reasonable means before reprogramming. If the institution fails to verify the consumer's identity, the consumer is not liable for any unauthorized transfers. It would not be permissible to issue the unsolicited debit card and PIN to a consumer if they may be used immediately, even if the institution instructs the consumer not to use the card and PIN until there has been validation.

III. Liability of Consumer for Unauthorized Transfers (§205.6)

A. **General Rule.**   In general, a consumer is liable for unauthorized electronic fund transfers only if certain requirements regarding initial disclosures have been met. (§205.6(a)). Further, as a general rule, the amount of the consumer's liability does not exceed $50. Under certain circumstances, essentially where the consumer fails to notify the financial institution within two business days after learning of the loss or theft of the access device, the consumer may be liable for up to $500. Finally, the consumer's liability may be unlimited if the consumer fails to report within sixty (60) days of transmittal of the periodic statement any unauthorized electronic fund transfer that appears on that statement.

B. **Conditions to Liability.**

1. The consumer is liable for unauthorized transfers involving the consumer's account only if all of the following have occurred:

    (a) The access device is an *accepted access device* [an access device becomes an "accepted access device" when the consumer requests and receives, or signs, or uses the access device, or requests validation of an access device issued on an unsolicited basis §205.2(a)(2)];

    (b) The institution has provided a means to identify the consumer to whom the access device was issued [the regulation refers to signature, photograph, fingerprint or electronic or mechanical confirmation, but this also includes a PIN];

    (c) The institution has given written disclosures to the consumer of the following matters:

        (i)   notice of the consumer's liability for unauthorized transfers;

        (ii) the telephone number and address of the person to be notified concerning a possible unauthorized transfer; and

        (iii) the institution's business days [the term "business day" means any day on which the offices of the institution are open for carrying on *substantially all* business functions. §205.2(d)].

E

2. A specific agreement between the consumer and the institution limiting the consumer's liability would override any higher limits allowed by Reg. E, as would any applicable state law which limited the consumer's liability.

C. Amount of Liability.

1. The rules and exceptions to the rules for liability for unauthorized transfers are relatively complicated. They are summarized below. In the event of any questions, however, you should refer to Regulation E itself.

2. Unless an exception applies, the consumer is liable for the amount of the transfers that take place before *notice to the institution* [this term has a specific meaning, discussed below], but not more than $50.

3. The first exception is for the consumer's failure to give notice within two business days. If the consumer fails to give *notice to the institution* within two business days after learning of the loss or theft of the access device, the consumer's liability does not exceed the *lesser* of

(a) $500; or

(b) the sum of (1) $50 or the amount of unauthorized transfers occurring before the close of the two business days, whichever is less, and (2) the amount of unauthorized transfers which would not have occurred but for the failure of the consumer to notify the institution, and which occur after 2 business days and before notice is given.

For example, if the consumer fails to notify the financial institution within two (2) business days after learning of the loss, or theft of the card, the consumer's liability will not exceed $500 (unless the exception described below applies). He or she may then be liable for up to $50 of unauthorized transfers in the first two (2) business days, and the full amount of any other transfers occurring after the two (2) business days. To illustrate this point, if there were $125 of unauthorized transfers in the first two (2) days, after the consumer learns of the loss, and $600 worth of unauthorized transfers thereafter (which would not have occurred but for the failure of the consumer to notify the institution), then the consumer's liability is capped at $50 for the first two days, plus an additional $450 for the transfers after the two (2) days (because of the overall cap of $500), for a total of $500.

4. The second exception is for the consumer's failure to report, within sixty (60) days of transmittal of the periodic statement, any unauthorized transfer that appears on the statement. In that situation, the consumer's liability has no dollar limit, but it cannot exceed the sum of:

(a) the lesser of $50 or the amount of the unauthorized transfers that appear on that statement or occur during that sixty (60) day period; plus

(b) the unauthorized transfers occurring after the close of the sixty (60) days and before notice is given to the financial institution and which would not have occurred but for the consumer's failure to give notice.

5. Both exceptions may apply in the same situation.

6. If there is a delay in giving notice to the institution because of "extenuating circumstances" then the time periods "shall be extended to a reasonable time." §205.6(b)(4).

D. **Notice to Financial Institution.** Section 205.6(b)(5) defines what constitutes "notice to the financial institution." Notice can be written or oral, and its effectiveness does not depend on whether any particular person in fact receives the information. In fine bureaucratic fashion, notice is also given when no notice is given, that is, when the institution "becomes aware of circumstances" that "lead to a reasonable belief" that unauthorized transfers have been made.

E. **Examples.** Section 205.6 in the Commentary gives useful examples explaining possible combinations of liability provisions.

IV. Initial Disclosure of Terms and Conditions (§205.7)

A. **Timing and Form of Disclosures.**

1. The initial disclosures required by §205.7 must be given before the first electronic fund transfer is made involving an account.

2. The disclosures must be in a readily understandable written statement that the consumer may retain.

B. **Content of Disclosures.** The initial disclosures must include the following provisions. However, the disclosures need only be given " as applicable," so that if, for example, preauthorized electronic fund transfers are not part of the program, then that disclosure need not be given. [Appendix A to the Regulation contains a model form for each of these disclosures.]

1. A summary of the consumer's liability under §205.6.;

2. The telephone number and address of the person to be notified when an unauthorized transfer has been made;

3. The institution's business days;

4. The type of transfers the consumer an make, and any limitations on the frequency and dollar amount of the transfers;

5. Any charges for the transfers;

6. A summary of the consumer's right to receive documentation of transfers;

7. A summary of the consumer's right to stop payment of a preauthorized electronic fund transfer and the procedure for initiating a stop payment order;

8   A summary of the institution's liability for failure to make or stop certain transfers;

9. The circumstances under which the financial institution in the ordinary course of business will disclose information to third parties concerning the consumer's account; and

10. A notice concerning error resolution procedures and the consumer's rights under them. [There is a precise form of this notice in Model Form A-3 of Appendix A.]

V.   Notice of Changes in Terms and Error Resolution Procedures (§205.8)

A. **Changes in Terms.**   An institution must mail or deliver a written notice to the consumer at least twenty-one (21) days before the effective date of any change in a term or condition required to be disclosed under §205.7(a) if the change would result in increased fees or charges, increased liability for the consumer, fewer types of available electronic fund transfers, or stricter limitations on the frequency or dollar amounts or transfers. [There are some exceptions if the security of the account would be jeopardized by prior notice.]

B. **Error Resolution Notice.**   A Standard form of error resolution notice must either be mailed once each calender year to the consumer, or a standard notice can be included on each periodic billing statement. Model forms of these annual and periodic notices are set forth in Appendix A.

VI.   Documentation of Transfers (§205.9(a))

A. **Timing of Receipts.**   At the time an electronic fund transfer is initiated at an *electronic terminal,* the institution must make available to the consumer a written receipt of the transfer. A financial institution may arrange for a third party such as a merchant to make the receipt available.

B. **Content of Receipt.**   The following information must appear on the receipt, as applicable:

1. The amount of the transfer;

2. The calender date of the transfer;

3. The type of transfer and the type of the account to or from which funds are transferred; however, the type of account need not be identified if the access device may access only one account at that terminal;

4. A number or code that identifies the consumer's account, or the access device;

5. The location of the terminal (see §205.9(b)(1)(iv), described below at VII.B.1.(d)); and

6. The name of any third party to or from whom funds are transferred.

VII.   Periodic Statements (§205.9(b))

A. **Timing.**   For any account to or from which electronic fund transfers can be made, a periodic statement must be mailed or delivered to the consumer for each monthly cycle in which an electronic fund transfer has occurred. A periodic statement must be mailed at least quarterly if no transfer has occurred.

B. **Content.**   The periodic statement must include the following information, as applicable:

1. For each electronic fund transfer occurring during the cycle:

(a) the amount of the transfer;

(b) the date the transfer was credited or debited to the consumer's account;

(c) the type of transfer and the type of the consumer account to or from which funds were transferred;

(d) for each transfer initiated by the consumer at an electronic terminal, either (x) the location that appeared on the receipt or, ( ) if an identification on the receipt was used, that identification and *one* of the following descriptions of the terminal's location:

(i) the address or intersection;

(ii) a generally accepted name for a location, the city and the state; or

(iii) the name of the entity at whose place of business the terminal is located or which owns or operates the terminal, the city and the state [if all the terminals owned or operated by the institution are in the same city, then the city and state may be omitted];

(e) the name of any third party to or from whom funds were transferred;

2. The account number;

3. Fees or charges imposed against the account for transfers, or the right to make transfers, or for account maintenance;

4. The balance in the consumer's account at the beginning and at the end of the statement period;

5. The address and telephone number to be used for inquiry or notice of errors [unless this is on the notice of error resolution procedures given under §205.8(b)]; and

6. A certain telephone number if preauthorized transfers are allowed.

VIII.   Error Resolution Procedures (§205.11)

A. **Definition of Error.**   An *error* includes the obvious items such as unauthorized transfers or transfers in an incorrect amount, and also includes a consumer's request for documentation or for additional information or clarification concerning an electronic fund transfer. However, a routine inquiry about the balance in an account, or a request for duplicate copies of documentation, is not an "error".

B. **Notice of Error.**   A notice of error is an oral or written notice from the consumer that is received by the institution [which can require that it be received at a specific phone number or address] no later than 60 days after the institution transmitted the relevant periodic statement or provided the relevant documentation, and which enables the institution to identify the consumer, and which gives the reasons for the consumer's belief that an error has occurred. The institution may request written confirmation of an oral notice.

C. **Error Investigation.**

1. The institution must promptly investigate the alleged error, determine whether it occurred, and advise the consumer of that determination within ten (10) (may be twenty (20); see item 4 below) business days.

2. The financial institution may take up to forty-five (45) (may be ninety (90); see item 4 below) calendar days to determine whether the error occurred and then transmit the results of its investigation, if the institution satisfies several requirements:

   (a) the institution provisionally recredits the consumer's account, as appropriate;

   (b) the institution promptly advises the consumer of the recrediting and of the fact that the consumer will have use of the recredited funds until the determination of whether the error occurred;

   (c) the institution gives the consumer full use of the funds which were provisionally recredited; and

(d)   if the institution determines that no error occurred, then the institution must give notice of the debiting of the account.

3.   The institution need not provisionally recredit a consumer's account if it requires, but does not receive, timely written confirmation of oral notice of an error.

4.   If the notice of error involved an electronic fund transfer resulting from a point of sale debit card transaction [which will be the case in most situations involving campus debit cards], then the applicable time periods referred to above are twenty (20) business days and ninety (90) calendar days, respectively. §205.11(c)(3).

D.   Extent of Required Investigation.

1.   The institution must review its own records regarding an alleged error. This will be sufficient unless there is an agreement between the institution and the third party to which or from which the transfer was made, and in that event, then the records of the third party must also be reviewed.

2.   If the institution is willing to make the correction requested by the consumer, it may do so without investigation.

E.   Procedures After Determining That an Error Has Occurred.   If the institution determines that an error occurred, then it must correct the error within one (1) business day.

F.   Procedures If No Error Occurred.

1.   If the institution determines that no error occurred, then the institution must notify the consumer of its findings within the time period required by §205.11(c). The notice must include a notice of the consumer's right to request additional documents on which the institution relied in making its determination.

2.   If the institution had provisionally credited the amount of the error, and then reverses that credit after determining that no error occurred, then notice must be given to the consumer of that fact, and the institution must honor for a short period of time certain paper instruments or preauthorized transfers.

IX.   Relation to State Law (§205.12)

A.   Preemption.   The Federal Reserve Board has the authority to determine whether federal law preempts any contrary state law. Standards are provided in §205.12 for determining when a state law is inconsistent with federal law, thereby permitting the Federal Reserve Board to determine that preemption has occurred.

B. **State Law Issues.**   There may be laws in a particular state which also have an impact on the issuance of debit cards. Michigan, for example, has an electronic fund transfers act. If these laws provide more benefits to the consumer than federal law, then they may supersede the federal law. Furthermore, state laws may not only regulate electronic fund transfers, but may also limit the ability of an institution to offer services of this type. Some commentators have, for example, questioned whether some of the proposed activities could require the institution to be regulated under state banking laws.

X.   Multiple Institutions (§205.14)

Section 205.14 provides for the division of responsibilities between a service providing institution [such as the college] and a "account holding institution" [such as a bank], where the college issues an access device to a consumer to be used for initiating transfers to or from the consumer's account held by the bank. This section identifies ways in which the various disclosure requirements can be made and who must make them.

XI.   Enforcement and Penalties

A. **Enforcement.**   The Federal Reserve Board drafted Reg. E and continues to make proposed changes and interpretations of Reg. E. Its legal staff is a source of information about the current view of the Federal Reserve Board (or at least its legal staff) regarding enforcement of the Regulation. However, colleges and universities are subject to regulation and enforcement activity by the Federal Trade Commission.

B. **Penalties.**   The penalties for violating Regulation E are set forth in the Act, not the Regulation. Sections 1693m and 1693n provide for both civil and criminal penalties when a financial institution fails to comply with Regulation E.

C. **Civil Liability General Rule.**   Section 1693m provides for civil liability for any person who fails to comply with the provisions of the Act and Regulation E. A financial institution which fails to comply with the Act and Regulation E is liable to the consumer for the amount equal to the sum of:

1.   Any actual damage sustained by the consumer as a result of such failure; and

2.   For *Individual Actions*, an amount not less than $100 nor greater than $1,000; or

3.   For *Class Actions*, the amount is under the discretion of the court except:

    (a)   there is no minimum recovery applicable to each member of the class; and

    (b)   the total recovery for the class is limited to $500,000 or 1 per centum of

L

the net worth of the defendant financial institution.

4. A financial institution is also liable for the cost of the action, and reasonable attorney's fees for the consumer's attorney.

5. In determining the amount of an award under Section 1693m the court will consider a number of factors including:

(a) For *Individual Actions* the frequency of and persistence of noncompliance; the nature of such noncompliance; and the extent to which noncompliance was intentional.

(b) For *Class Actions* the court will consider the frequency of noncompliance; the nature of such noncompliance; the resources of the defendant financial institution; the number of persons adversely affected; and the extent of noncompliance.

D. Exceptions.

1. It is important to note that a financial institution which would otherwise be liable under section 1693m, may not be held liable if the compliance was not intentional, but rather due to a bona fide error. However, such error must have occurred notwithstanding the maintenance of procedures already in place at the financial institution which were adopted to comply with Regulation E and the Act. Moreover, a financial institution would not be liable for good faith reliance on any rule, regulation, or interpretation issued by or on the behalf of the Federal Reserve Board, or for any failure to make a disclosure *if* the financial institution utilized a model clause or form issued by the Federal Reserve Board. §1693m(d).

2. **Notification to Consumer Prior to Action.** A financial institution would not be liable under section 1693m if prior to the institution of an action it:

(a) notifies the customer about the noncompliance;

(b) complies with Regulation E and the Act;

(c) makes an adjustment to the consumer's account; and

(d) pays actual damages to the consumer.

E. Action in Bad Faith. If a consumer is *unsuccessful* in his or her action against a financial institution *and* a court concludes that the action was brought in bad faith for purposes of harassment, the court must award the financial institution reasonable attorney's fees.

F. Criminal Liability General Rule. A financial institution may also be criminally liable to a consumer if it:

1. Knowingly or willfully gives false or inaccurate information to a consumer;

2. Fails to provide the required disclosure information to a consumer; or

3. Otherwise fails to comply with Regulation E and the Act. §1693n.

4. A person who is criminally liable under the Act will be fined not more than $5,000 or imprisoned for not more than one (1) year, or both.

5. Section 1693n of the Act also provides for criminal penalties for various violations of the Act involving the knowing, unlawful, fraudulent and intentional transportation or use of counterfeit, lost, stolen, altered, forged or fictitious debt cards in interstate commerce. The penalty for these acts will not exceed $10,000 or ten (10) years imprisonment, or both. §1693n(b).

SAMPLE REQUEST FOR PROPOSAL (RFP)

The following RFP is provided by Oregon State University as a sample RFP for campus card systems. It is to be used for study purposes only, as each RFP must be written for the exclusive needs of the college or university sending out its "Request for Proposal."

OREGON STATE UNIVERSITY

REQUEST FOR PROPOSAL

RFP K98-2

Campus ID Card Transaction Management System

ADMINISTRATOR: Oregon State University

BUYER: Kelly Scherer
Phone: (541) 737-2067
FAX: (541) 737-2170

ISSUE DATE: February 25, 1998

CLOSING DATE: March 25, 1998, 2:00 PM

NO LATE PROPOSALS WILL BE ACCEPTED

SUBMITTAL LOCATION

Oregon State University Purchasing
Attn: Shannon Fanourakis/Kelly Scherer
644 SW 13th Street
Corvallis, Oregon 97333-4238

INDEX

SCHEDULE OF EVENTS

RFP released   February 25, 1998
Request for Clarifications Due   March 12, 1998
RFP Closing   March 25, 1998, 2:00 PM
Project completion   Not later than August 15, 1998

PART I - INTRODUCTION AND
SUPPLEMENTAL INFORMATION REGARDING BIDDING

This is a Request for Proposal (RFP) to acquire a complete online one-card campus ID Card transaction management system.

Oregon State University's ID card production and campus card transaction management program is administered by the ID Center, which is under the jurisdiction of Student Affairs, and Memorial Union-Student Involvement.

Currently, the ID Center operates an all-campus ID card system under a 5-year lease, which expires in 1998. OSU uses the system for card transactions in Dining Centers (meal plans), retail dining and fast food locations (debit and credit point plans), privilege verification at various facilities (recreational centers, athletic events, etc.), door access (only one door). The ID Center also operates a digital imaging system for card production, running separately from the transaction processing system.

PROJECT OBJECTIVES

Provide electronic capture of digital photographs of OSU students, staff, faculty, and visitors.
Provide printed and encoded identification cards using digital photographs.
Store digital photographs and data records for OSU students, staff, faculty, and visitors on a database shared by the campus card transaction processing system.
Continue using the ID card design we currently have. Mass re-carding of the university is not a goal in this project.
Provide encoding services, encoding ID numbers on magnetic stripe of card.
Provide Card-based purchase and verification operations consisting of online authorization of a transaction based on privilege, account balance, time, and location restrictions through real-time communications with the network of card readers.
Continue providing card-based purchase and verification services to OSU students, staff and faculty for the following applications:
Point-of-sale debit and credit for dining
Meal plans for summer conferences and visiting groups
Credit accounts for meal plans
Privilege verification for activity access
Door access control and alarm monitoring
Library check-out using 3 of 9 bar code
Digital imaging ID card production
8. Begin (over the next 5 years) providing card purchase and verification services for the following applications:
More door access control locations, interfacing with HID Proximity card readers, primarily at Residence Hall outer doors
Vending machine purchases with debit account
Copy purchases from copy machines with debit or credit account
Departmental service/supply fees with debit or credit account
Remote, unattended deposit stations for opening, adding to debit accounts and debit card purchases
f. Networked laser printer usage and payment

QUESTIONS AND REQUEST FOR CHANGE:
All clarifications regarding technical information, and procedural, contractual requirements or other issues, as well, all technical, contractual or procedural request for change must be submitted, in writing, no later than the date and time listed in the schedule of events to the names and address listed below. All requests for change must be received in writing. Proposers must

take note that OSU is not allowed to consider exceptions to the specifications or terms and conditions after the RFP period has closed. If you have an exception or a concern with anything in this RFP, you must raise that issue, in writing, by the deadline date for Requests for Change, listed in the RFP. Requests submitted to other than the person(s) listed below will not be considered. Requests for change may be submitted via facsimile.

> Kelly Scherer, Buyer
> Oregon State University, Purchasing Department
> 644 SW 13th Street
> Corvallis, Oregon 97333-4238
> Voice: (541) 737-2067   Fax: (541) 737-2170

CHANGE OR MODIFICATION: Any change or modification to the specifications or the procurement process will be in the form of an addendum to the RFP and will be made available to bidders.

PRE-BID CONFERENCE

There will be no pre-bid conference.

PROPOSAL SUBMISSIONS: Proposers shall submit ONE (1) ORIGINAL copy of all proposal/bid pages that request information from the proposer/bidder AND SIX (6) PHOTO COPIES of same pages to the location listed on page 1 of this RFP by the time listed on page 1 of this RFP.

Original shall be marked "ORIGINAL". Original copy shall contain original signatures on any pages where it is requested. Additionally, submit six (6) copies of any illustrated literature or other technical matter included by-way of explanation of your proposal/bid.

NEW EQUIPMENT REQUIRED: For this RFP, all equipment must be new. Refurbished equipment is not acceptable.

METHOD OF AWARD: Contract award shall be made to the highest-ranked proposer. Rankings shall be assigned as described in the RFP. OSU reserves the right to not award a contract if it is determined to be in the best interest of the University to do so.

REQUIRED INFORMATION: Bidder must complete all applicable information and provide all information requested in RFP. Failure to comply may be grounds for proposal rejection.

Bidder shall also name its Contract Administrator, an individual's name, title and phone number, who is assigned the responsibility of answering questions and resolving problems.

PRE-AWARD DEMONSTRATION OF EQUIPMENT: Upon request, and at the option of OSU, the apparent successful bidder shall demonstrate the bid equipment offered at a location and time designated by OSU. The apparent low bidder shall supply all necessary equipment, supplies and labor for this demonstration. Demonstration shall be to the effect to show that the offered items meet all mandatories and specifications given in the bid. If the apparent successful proposer who, during the pre-award demonstration, fails to demonstrate compliance with all mandatories specified in the bid, shall be rejected.

METHOD OF AWARD: Contract award shall be made to the highest-ranked proposer. Rankings shall be assigned as described in the RFP. OSU reserves the right to not award a contract if it is determined to be in the best interest of the University to do so.

PROPOSAL OPENING PROCEDURE: All proposals received in response to this RFP shall be opened at the scheduled time and date. Bidders who attend the opening will be informed only of the names and bidders submitting proposals. No other information will be available.

PART II - GENERAL INFORMATION

Oregon State University (OSU) reserves the right, for good and just cause, to reject any or all proposals received as a result of this Request for Proposals (RFP), or upon a finding that it is in the public interest to do so.

II-1 Protest of Requirements: Protests of the technical requirements or requests for non-substantive or procedural changes to the Contractual Provisions contained in Part III of the RFP, shall be in writing and delivered to the OSU Purchasing Department prior to the deadline specified in the schedule of events. Protests of technical or contractual requirements shall include the reason for the protest, and any proposed changes to the requirements.

The purpose of this requirement is to permit OSU to correct, prior to the opening of proposals, technical or contractual requirements that may be unlawful, improvident, or which unjustifiably may restrict competition. This requirement will allow OSU to make needed corrections through the issuance of an addendum, prior to the opening of proposals. This will help eliminate the waste of time which is inherent in protests and in the possible rejection of all proposals. In order to have their complaints considered, bidders must submit them within the time established in the RFP. OSU shall not at any subsequent time consider a bidder's objections to technical requirements or specifications unless those objections have been timely presented to the OSU Purchasing Department under this Section.

OSU will consider all requested changes and, if appropriate, amend the RFP.

Envelopes containing requests for change or protests of solicitation specifications or contract provisions shall be marked as follows:

Solicitation Specification (or Contract Provisions) Request for Change (or Protest) and Solicitation Document t Number (or Other Identification).

II-2 Addenda: If any part of this RFP is amended, addenda will be provided to all bidders who received the initial RFP.

II-3 Proposal Preparation and Submission: Proposals and pricing information shall be prepared by typewriter or in ink and shall be signed in ink by an authorized representative of the company. Alterations or erasures shall be initialed in ink by the person signing the RFP. AT LEAST ONE PROPOSAL SUBMITTED BY BIDDER MUST BEAR AN ORIGINAL SIGNATURE. FAILURE TO SUBMIT A PROPOSAL BEARING AN ORIGINAL SIGNATURE WILL RESULT IN REJECTION OF THE PROPOSAL. No oral, telegraphic, telephone or facsimile proposals will be accepted.

Proposals must be complete. Incomplete proposals cannot be considered and cannot be supplemented by submissions delivered after the closing time and date of the RFP.

Proposals must be submitted in sealed package(s) or envelope(s). To ensure proper identification and handling, all package(s) or envelope(s) must be clearly marked with the RFP Number and date and time of closing. Pricing information must be submitted in a separate sealed package, and must be clearly marked "Pricing Information". Pricing must not be included with the Proposal.

Proposals and pricing information must be received and time-stamped by the OSU Purchasing Department (unless otherwise specified) prior to scheduled RFP closing date. Late proposals and/or modifications shall not be considered.

Proposals received in response to this RFP shall be opened at the OSU Purchasing Department (unless otherwise specified), at the scheduled closing time. Bidders who attend the opening will be informed only of the names of bidders submitting proposals.

No other information will be provided at that time.

II-4 Alternate Proposals: Bidders may submit more than one proposal. All proposals must comply with the requirements of the RFP except that additional proposals may incorporate, by reference, repetitive information which is provided in the complete proposal.

II-5 Evaluation of Proposals: Proposals will be evaluated by a committee consisting of representatives of OSU.

The evaluation will determine if the proposal meets the technical requirements, and the extent to which they meet the desirable features of the RFP. The following process will be used:

A.   Proposals will be evaluated for completeness and compliance with the requirements of this RFP. Those proposals that are incomplete will be rejected.

B.   Proposals considered complete will be evaluated to determine if they comply with the administrative, contractual and technical requirements of the RFP. If the proposal is unclear, bidders may be asked to provide written clarification. Those proposals that do not meet all requirements will be rejected.

C.   At the option of OSU, at any point in the evaluation process, the bidder may be required to demonstrate their ability or give verbal presentation to clarify their proposal.

D.   Proposals that meet all requirements will be evaluated on desirable features. At the option of OSU, bidders may be asked to provide written clarification and/or demonstrate their proposed features to aid the Evaluation Committee in awarding desirable points to the proposal. Points shall be assigned for desirables based on their value to OSU. Maximum point allocations for desirables are contained in Part V.

E.   After points have been assigned by the evaluators to each bidder's proposal, prices will be opened and evaluated as indicated in the evaluation matrix contained in the RFP. Total cost shall be determined as specified in the RFP.

F.   The findings of the Evaluation Committee will be summarized and the summary and award recommendation will be forwarded to the OSU Purchasing Department.

G.   The OSU Purchasing Department will review the recommendation and approve or reject the Committee's selection.

II-6 Post-Selection Review: OSU will name an apparent successful bidder. Identification of the "apparent successful bidder" is procedural only and creates no right in the named bidder to award of the contract. Competing bidders shall be notified in writing of the identity of the apparent successful bidder and shall be given fourteen (14) calendar days to review the RFP file and evaluation report at the OSU Purchasing Department. Any questions or concerns about, or protests of, the evaluation process must be in writing and must be delivered to the OSU Purchasing Department within fourteen (14) calendar days after the date of the letter identifying the apparent successful bidder.

Within a reasonable time following the end of this fourteen (14) day protest period, OSU will consider all protests received, if any, and:

        (a)   pursuant to OAR 137-30-104(4), reject all protests and proceed with final evaluation of the apparent successful bidder and, pending the satisfactory outcome of this final evaluation, enter into a contract with the named bidder; OR

(b)   pursuant to OAR 580-040-0277 and OAR 580-040-0280, sustain a meritorious protest(s) and reject the apparent successful bidder as nonresponsive, if such bidder is unable to demonstrate that its proposal complied with all material requirements of the solicitation and Oregon public procurement law; thereafter, OSU may name a new apparent successful bidder; OR

(c)   pursuant to OAR 137-30-102, reject all proposals and cancel the procurement.

II-7 Acceptance of Contractual Requirements: Failure of the selected bidder to execute a contract within 30 days after notification of award may result in cancellation of the award. This time period may be extended at the option of OSU.

In the event that charges result from the inclusion of some or all of the provisions of the contractual requirements of this RFP, such charges shall be included as part of the proposed total price.

The order of precedence of attachments to the final contract will generally be: (1) General Information - Part II; (2) Contractual section of the RFP - Part III; (3) the technical section and the Financial section of the RFP; (4) Bidder's proposal document; and (5) Bidder's official published specifications.

II-8 News Release: News releases pertaining to this acquisition will be made only with the prior written consent of OSU, and then only in coordination with OSU.

II-9 Public Records: This RFP and one copy of each original proposal received in response to it, together with copies of all documents pertaining to the award of a contract, shall be kept by the OSU Purchasing Department and made a part of a file or record which shall be open to public inspection. If a proposal contains any information that is considered a trade secret under ORS 192.501 (2), each sheet of such information must be marked with the following legend:

"This data constitutes a trade secret under ORS 192.501(2), and shall not be disclosed except in accordance with the Oregon Public Records Law, ORS Chapter 192."

The Oregon Public Records Law exempts from disclosure only bona fide trade secrets, and the exemption from disclosure applies only "unless the public interest requires disclosure in the particular instance." ORS 192.501(2). Therefore, non-disclosure of documents or any portion of a document submitted as part of a proposal may depend upon official or judicial determinations made pursuant to the Public Records Law.

The above restriction may not include cost or price information which must be open to public inspection.

II-10 Proprietary Function of OSU: This procurement is a proprietary function of OSU. OSU has and reserves the right to refuse to enter into a contract if OSU, based upon reasonable grounds, determines that the legitimate ends of OSU would not be served. Specifically, this right may be exercised if OSU does not believe that a given bidder can perform a contract, or for any reason set forth in ORS 580-040-0277, 580-040-0280 or 580-040-0285. OSU, at its option, may give the bidder notice, specifying the grounds for rejection, and allow the bidder 15 calendar days to respond in writing.

II-11 Investigation of References: OSU reserves the right to investigate the references and the past performance of any bidder with respect to its successful performance of similar projects, compliance with specifications and contractual obligations, its completion or delivery of a project on schedule, and its lawful payment of suppliers, sub-contractors, and workers. OSU may postpone the award or execution of the contract after the announcement of the apparent successful bidder in order to complete its investigation. OSU reserves its right to reject any proposal or to reject all proposals at any time prior to OSU's execution of a contract.

II-12 Prior Acceptance of Defective Proposals: Due to the limited resources of OSU, OSU generally will not completely review or analyze proposals which clearly fail to comply with the requirements of the RFP or which, in the opinion of OSU, are not the best proposals, nor will OSU generally investigate the references or qualifications of those who submit such proposals. Therefore, neither the release of a bidder's bid bond, the return of a proposal, or acknowledgment that the selection is complete, shall operate as a representation by OSU that an unsuccessful proposal was complete, sufficient, or lawful in any respect.

PART III - TERMS AND CONDITIONS

III-1 Definitions:

"Bidder" means the entity who prepares the proposal and will be listed as the contractor on the contract. For purposes of award of desirable points, "bidder" must provide the component, feature or characteristic within their own business, not the business of a represented manufacturer or other company.

"Contract" means the entire written agreement between the parties, including but not limited to the Invitation to Bid or Request for Proposal and its specifications, terms and conditions; solicitation instructions; solicitation addenda and contract amendments, if any; the contractor's proposal; and the purchase order or price agreement document;

"Contractor" means a person or organization with whom OSU has contracted for the provision of the service or services under this contract. The terms "Contractor" and "Seller" as used in the Uniform Commercial Code (ORS chapter 72) are synonymous;

"Department" means any institution, institution department or other political subdivision (as authorized) which is party to the contract.

"OARS" means the Administrative Rules adopted by the State of Oregon Board of Higher Education.

"ORS" means the Oregon Revised Statutes;

"OSU" means Oregon State University and is synonymous with "Buyer" as used in ORS Chapter 12. "OSU" also means other parties to the contract if the purchase is being made under a cooperative agreement;

"OSU Purchasing Department" means the Purchasing Department of the Property Management Department of Oregon State University acting for and through OSU.

III-2 Independent Contractor Status: The service or services to be rendered under this contract are those of an independent contractor. Contractor is not an officer, employee or agent of OSU as those terms are used in ORS 30.265.

III-3 Retirement System Status: Contractor is not a contributing member of the Public Employees' Retirement System and will be responsible for any federal or state taxes applicable to payment under this contract. Contractor will not be eligible for any benefits from these contract payments of federal Social Security, employment insurance, workers' compensation or the Public Employees' Retirement System, except as a self-employed individual.

III-4 Government Employment Status:

A.   If this payment is to be charged against federal funds, Contractor certifies that it is not currently employed by the federal government.

B.   Contractor certifies it is not an employee of OSU.

III-5 Assignment/Subcontract/Successors: Contractor shall not assign, sell, transfer, or subcontract rights, or delegate responsibilities under this contract, in whole or in part, without the prior written approval of the OSU Purchasing Department. No such written approval shall relieve Contractor of any obligations of this contract, and any transferee or subcontractor shall be considered the agent of Contractor. Contractor shall remain liable to OSU under the contract as if no such assignment, transfer, or subcontract had occurred. The provisions of this contract shall be binding upon and shall inure to the benefit of the parties to the contract and their respective successors and assigns.

III-6 Compliance With Applicable Laws: Contractor shall comply with all federal, state and local laws, codes, regulations and ordinances applicable to the provision of goods under this contract, including, without limitation, the provisions of ORS 279.312, 279.314, and 279.316 (1), as set forth below and the provisions of: (i) Title VI of the Civil Rights Act of 1964; (ii) Section V of the Rehabilitation Act of 1973; (iii) the Americans with Disabilities Act of 1990 (Pub L No. 101-336). ORS 659.425, and all amendments of and regulations and administrative rules established pursuant to those laws; and (iv) all other applicable requirements of federal and state civil rights and rehabilitation statutes, rules and regulations.

III-7 Governing Law: This Contract shall be governed and construed in accordance with the laws of the State of Oregon. Any claim, action, or suit between OSU and Contractor that arrived out of or relates to performance of this contract shall be brought and conducted solely and exclusively within the Circuit Court for Marion County, for the state of Oregon. Provided, however that if any such claim, action, or suit may be brought only in federal forum, it shall be brought and conducted solely and exclusively within the United States District Court for the State of Oregon.

III-8 Attorney Fees: In the event a lawsuit of any kind is instituted on behalf of OSU to collect any payment due or to obtain performance of any kind under this contract, Contractor shall pay such additional sums as the court may adjudge for reasonable attorney fees plus all costs and disbursements at trial and on any appeal.

III-9 Force Majeure: Neither party to this contract shall be held responsible for delay or default caused by fire, riot, acts of God and/or war which is beyond the party's reasonable control. OSU may terminate this contract upon written notice after determining such delay or default will reasonably prevent successful performance of this contract.

III-10 Hold Harmless: Contractor shall indemnify, defend and hold harmless OSU and its departments, officers, employees, agents and members, from all claims, suits or actions of any nature arising out of or related to the activities of Contractor, its officers, subcontractors, agents or employees under this contract.

III-11 Severability: If any provision of this contract is declared by a court of competent jurisdiction to be illegal or in conflict with any law, the validity of the remaining terms and provisions shall not be affected; and the rights and obligations of the parties shall be construed and enforced as if the contract did not contain the particular provision held to be invalid.

III-12 Access To Records: The Contractor shall maintain all fiscal records relating to this contract in accordance with generally accepted accounting principle and shall maintain any other records relating to this contract in such a manner as to clearly document Contractor's performance hereunder. OSU and its departments, the Secretary of State Audits Division, the federal government and their duly authorized representatives shall have access to such fiscal records and to all other books, documents, papers, plans and writings of Contractor which relate to this contract, to perform examination, and audits and make excerpts and transcripts.

III-13 Waiver: Failure of OSU to enforce any provision of this contract shall not be a waiver or relinquishment by OSU of its right to such performance in the future nor of the right to enforce any other provisions of this contract.

III-14 Amendments: The terms of this contract shall not be waived, altered, modified, supplemented or amended in any manner whatsoever without prior written approval of the OSU Purchasing Department.

III-15 Payment Of Contractor's Obligations: Contractor agrees to make payment promptly, as due, to all persons furnishing services, equipment or supplies to Contractor for the performance of work under this contract. If Contractor fails, neglects or refuses to pay such claims as they become due, the proper officer(s) representing OSU, after ascertaining that the claims are just, due and payable, may pay the claims and charge the amount of the payment against funds due or to become due Contractor under this contract. The payment of claims in this manner shall not relieve Contractor with respect to any unpaid claims.

III-16 Nondiscrimination: Contractor shall comply with all applicable requirements of federal and state civil rights and rehabilitation statutes, rules and regulations.

III-17 Dual Payment: Contractor shall not be compensated for work performed under this contract from any OSU department other than the department which is a party to this contract.

III-18 Award To Foreign Contractor: If Contractor is not domiciled in or registered to do business in the State of Oregon, Contractor shall promptly provide to the Oregon Department of Revenue and the Secretary of State Corporation Division all information required by those agencies relative to this contract. OSU shall withhold final payment under this contract until Contractor has met this requirement.

III-19 Payment: Payment for completion of OSU contracts are normally made within 30 days following the date the service is provided or the date the invoice is received, whichever is later. After 45 days, Contractor may assess overdue account charges up to a maximum rate of two-thirds of one percent per month on the outstanding balance (ORS 293.462).

III-20 Breach Of Contract: Should Contractor breach any of the provisions of this contract, OSU reserves the right to cancel this contract upon written notice to contractor. Contractor shall be liable for any and all damages incidental and consequential suffered by OSU as the result of Contractor's breach of contract by Contractor. In the event of repeated breach of public and/or private contracts, Contractor shall be subject to disqualification as a bidder on OSU contracts.

OSU shall have the option to terminate the contract at any time for performance that is not in compliance with all the instructions and specifications stated herein. Unsatisfactory performance shall include, but not be limited to: unacceptable quality of item(s), mis-shipment of ordered quantities, and non-availability of items. In the event that the Contractor's performance is deemed unsatisfactory, OSU shall provide a statement of complaint, detailing specifics to the Contractor. Three (3) letters of complaint will constitute a breach of contract and OSU may, at its option, cancel the contract.

III-21 Warranties: Unless otherwise stated, all equipment shall be new and current model and shall carry full factory warranties. Contractor warrants all goods delivered to be free from defects in labor, material and manufacture and to be in compliance with bid specifications. All implied or expressed warranty provisions of the Uniform Commercial Code (ORS chapter 72) are incorporated in this Contract. All warranties shall run to OSU.

III-22 Safety And Health Requirements: Equipment and services supplied shall comply with all federal Occupational Safety and Health Admin. (OSHA) requirements and with all Oregon safety and health requirements, including those of the State of Oregon Workers' Compensation Department.

III-23 Inspections: Goods furnished under this Contract shall be subject to inspection and test by OSU at times and places determined by OSU. If OSU finds goods furnished to be incomplete or not in compliance with bid specifications, OSU may reject the goods and require Contractor to either correct them without charge or deliver them at a reduced price which is equitable under the circumstances. If Contractor is unable or refuses to correct such goods within a time deemed reasonable by OSU, OSU may cancel the order in whole or in part. Nothing in this paragraph shall adversely affect OSU's rights as buyer, including the rights and remedies associated with revocation of acceptance under ORS 72.6080.

III-24 Merger: This contract constitutes the entire contract between the parties. There are no understandings, oral or written, not specified herein regarding this contract. No amendment, consent, or waiver of terms of this contract shall bind either party unless in writing and signed by all parties. Any such amendment, consent, or waiver shall be effective only in the specific instance and for the specific purpose given. Contractor, by the signature hereto of its authorized representative, acknowledges having read and understood the contract and contractor agrees to be bound by its terms and conditions.

III-25 Insurance Terms And Conditions:

COMPREHENSIVE AUTO LIABILITY INSURANCE AND GENERAL LIABILITY INSURANCE: Contractor shall obtain, at Contractor's expense, and keep in effect during the term of this purchase order or contract, Comprehensive Auto Liability and General Liability Insurance. Such insurance policy is to be issued by an insurance company authorized to do business in the State of Oregon. Contractual, product and completed operations liability combined single limit per occurrence shall not be less than $1,000,000, or the equivalent. Each annual aggregate limit shall not be less than $1,000,000, when applicable. OSU and the Oregon State System of Higher Education, their officers, employees and agents shall be included as additional insured in said insurance policy.

WORKERS' COMPENSATION: The Contractor, its subcontractors, if any, and all employers providing work, labor or materials under this Contract are subject employers under the Oregon Workers' Compensation law and shall comply with ORS 656.017, which requires them to provide workers' compensation coverage that satisfies Oregon law for all their subject workers.

PRIMARY COVERAGE: Insurance carried by Contractor under this purchase order or contract shall be the primary coverage and OSU's insurance is excess and solely for damages or losses for which OSU is responsible.

CERTIFICATES OF INSURANCE: As evidence of the insurance coverages required by this contract, the contractor shall furnish Certificate(s) of Insurance to OSU, Purchasing Department, upon request. The Certificate(s) will specify all of the parties who are Additional Insureds (or Loss Payees). Insurance coverages required under this contract shall be obtained from acceptable insurance companies or entities. The contractor shall be financially responsible for all deductibles, self-insured retentions and/or self-insurance included hereunder.

NOTICE OF CANCELLATION OR CHANGE: There shall be no cancellation, material change, potential exhaustion of aggregate limits or intent not to renew insurance coverage(s) without 30 days' written notice from the contractor or its insurer(s) to OSU, Purchasing Department. Any failure to comply with the reporting provisions of this insurance, except for the potential exhaustion of aggregate limits, shall not affect the coverage(s) provided to OSU Purchasing.

NOTE: Contractor shall ensure any/all subcontractors comply with insurance requirements. OSU reserves the right to obtain subcontractor's insurance certificates at any time during the contract period.

III-26 Necessary Components: Contractor shall deliver and install the equipment and shall provide any component, hardware or part necessary for proper installation and operation even though that item is not specifically described in the bid specifications. Bidders shall include these costs in the bid price.

III-27 Equipment Relocation: OSU may relocate any equipment ordered under this contract based on their needs. Written notice of such shall be provided to the contractor. Any such relocation shall not void warranty or maintenance coverage.

PART IV - PROPOSAL FORMAT AND CONTENTS

Proposals must provide a concise description of the bidder's ability to satisfy the requirements of the RFP with emphasis on completeness and clarity of contents.

Pages should be numbered consecutively and a set of tabs inserted to identify each section of the proposal, such as: "A.1 Cover Letter", "A.2 Contractual Acceptance", etc.. All binders, reference materials, and other documents should be clearly labeled or otherwise identified and referenced in a clear and consistent manner throughout the proposal.

OSU shall not be liable for any costs incurred in the preparation and presentation of proposals.

By proposal submission, bidders agree to all requirements, terms and conditions contained in the Request for Proposal. After determining that a proposal meets and satisfies the written mandatory requirements stated in the RFP, the comparative assessment of the relative benefits of the proposal in relation to the published evaluation criteria shall be made by using the professional judgment by a Proposal Evaluation Board. The award of a contract resulting from this RFP shall be based on the best proposal received in accordance with the evaluation criteria stated in the RFP.

After an initial screening process, a technical question and answer conference or interview may be conducted between the bidder and OSU, if deemed necessary, to clarify or verify the bidder's proposal and to develop a comprehensive assessment of proposal.

OSU reserves the right to consider past performance, historical information and fact, whether gained from the bidder's proposal, question and answer conference, references, or any other source in the evaluation process.

The bidder is cautioned that it is the bidder's sole responsibility to submit information related to the evaluation categories, and that OSU is under no obligation to solicit such information if it is not included within the bidder's proposal. Failure by the bidder to submit such information may cause an adverse impact on the evaluation of the bidder's proposal.

Any award of a contract resulting from this RFP will be made only by written authorization in the form of a Notice to Proceed from OSU.

PROPOSAL FORMAT
A. GENERAL
1. Cover Letter: Cover letter containing a brief statement of the salient features of the proposal, including capabilities, experience, conclusions and recommendations.

2. Contractual Acceptance: Statement accepting all terms and conditions including Part III, Contractual Provisions.

3. Additional Information: Additional information which would aid in evaluating the proposal.

B. WRITTEN MANDATORY/DESIRABLE REQUIREMENTS

1. Response to Written Mandatories: Describe in detail, compliance with each mandatory requirement in Part V of the RFP. This may be in narrative form or by reference to other documentation or a combination of the two. It is preferable to retype the requirement from the RFP and respond directly below. Be sure to include in your responses for each requirement how your company can meet the qualifications. This information should include but not be limited to such items as company policies, program and service plans, etc.

2. Response to Desirables: Respond to each desirable in writing and in sufficient detail to allow the evaluation committee to assign points to the proposal. Respond in the same format as Item 1, Response to Written Mandatories.

C. PROPOSAL LITERATURE

1. Index: List all reference materials and other documents included with the Proposal.

D. FORMS

1. Appendices: Bidders must complete and return any forms referenced in this RFP.

E. PRICING PROPOSALS

Pricing Proposals must be submitted in a sealed envelope, separate from the proposal, and clearly identified with the RFP number, date and time of closing and the words "Pricing Information". Prices shall not be included in the Proposal.

PART V - MANDATORY REQUIREMENTS AND DESIRABLE FEATURES

GENERAL

The mandatory requirements and desirable features specified in this RFP are designed to assist the bidder in preparing a proposal to provide the products and services desired by OSSHE. The mandatory requirements presented specify the minimum capabilities and goods and services to be provided by the successful bidder. Additional desirable features which will be considered in the evaluation are also described. Bidders shall identify their costs associated with the mandatory and desirable requirements in the Pricing Section of their proposal. OSU reserves the right to incorporate all services and capabilities offered, at the discount structure proposed, in any resulting contract.

Mandatory requirements describe the minimal quality, service(s) and performance requirements that all proposals must fully comply with. Proposals that do not fully comply with all mandatory requirements of this RFP will be considered nonresponsive and will be rejected, which is why it is very important to request changes or protest requirements by the deadline given. If no changes are made to the RFP, and your response does not fully comply, it will be rejected. The written response to each mandatory must detail how their proposal meets the mandatory requirement. Only proposals that meet the mandatory requirements will be evaluated for desirable requirements.

The desirable requirements of this RFP specify features, characteristics or functions of the bidder which will further improve and enhance the level of performance, quality, service and or support. Response to desirable items are optional; however, points will be awarded based on how well the bidder's response meets each desirable item and its value to OSU. In addition, whichever features are proposed (and desirable points awarded for) will be incorporated into the resulting contract. Failure to meet the levels of performance and features proposed will be breach of contract and cause for contract termination.

Written responses to mandatory and desirable sections may be in written narrative form, by reference to other documentation included in your proposal or a combination of the two. Bidders are to indicate the document title, page number and specific paragraph(s) where the information is contained.

When responding, a simple "yes/no" answer to each item usually will not suffice. For mandatories, bidders must explain in sufficient detail how their proposed product(s) meet the requirement. The specific product, including version release, must be identified in the response. Bidder responses must comply with the intent of the mandatory requirements. If a bidder does provide a "yes" or "we comply" answer, the bidder will be held responsible for complying with that mandatory fully as the mandatory is interpreted in OSU's sole judgment if that bidder receives a contract. For desirables, bidders must provide sufficient information for OSU to judge the value of the product(s) and service(s) in relation to OSU's needs. Responses to desirables will be evaluated in terms of how well the bidder's product(s) provides the desired feature as well as evaluated competitively among the bidder responses based on how well each bidder's product(s) compares to others proposed in the context of OSU's needs.

SPECIFICATIONS AND REQUIREMENTS

MANDATORY REQUIREMENTS

ID CARD SPECIFICATION REQUIREMENTS
Strong, flexible PVC laminate with finish for direct printing with digital imaging system.
Dimensions: 2.125"x3.375"x0.031"nom.
Standard American Banking Association (ABA) Track II, high-energy magnetic stripe and encoding, customized to 2 tracks wide.
Encoding to include field for incremental lost card code.
Pre-printed on front with 4-color process, 1 color drop-in front (sample card enclosed).

2. HARDWARE
System must include an online transaction processing server and related equipment.
The system must be protected by an AC power line conditioner.
The system must be configured with a smart Uninterruptable Power Source (UPS) which shuts down the system gracefully on a loss of power and restarts automatically upon power restoration.
The system must be capable of holding 50,000 cardholder accounts and 130 card reader locations.
Disk I/O subsystem must be SCSI based.
Must incorporate an automatic backup system which does not shut the system down during backup.
The system must provide redundant storage of transaction data.
Must include a modem for remote diagnostics.
Must include stand-alone ABA encoders (2) to encode and re-encode existing cards.
The bidder's system must either include card readers which are programmed to communicate with the system transaction processing software, or must provide open architecture which allows use of currently marketed brands of card readers to communicate with the system transaction processing software. Details about card readers may be addressed on the attached Card Reader/Peripheral Equipment Worksheet.

3. COMMUNICATIONS
System remote workstations (PC) and printers must communicate with the on-line transaction processor via an Ethernet based network using the TCP/IP protocol.

b. The system must offer two options for card reader communications:
Dedicated point to point lines, and
An Ethernet based network using the TCP/IP protocol.

4. CARD READERS
All Card Reader models offered (Privilege Verification, POS, Vending, Door Access, Copier, and Remote Value Add-On Terminal) must have the following features:
A continuous swipe-through style card slot, which reads the encoded information on Track II of the ABA magnetic stripe on the ID card (exception for proximity access readers).
Must communicate with the transaction processor on line and in real time.
Must be capable of storing a minimum of 1,000 transactions off-line, which can be automatically uploaded to the transaction processor upon restoration of communication.
Must provide a visual response to operator and cardholder.

5. SOFTWARE
Bidder's proposed system and card readers must be Year 2,000 compliant.
Bidder's proposed system must include database management software (details can be addressed under the Desirable Features section of the RFP.
System must incorporate client workstation software with the following features:
Password protected access.
Modifies multiple cardholder accounts or plans with single command, based on common field values.
Executes system reports.
Modifies system configuration.
Performs all system administration operations (if password allows).
Provide for operator review of cardholder transactions

System Administration software must:
Assign operator/user security codes (passwords) to permit workstation access to designated program functions, workstations, printers, privileges, and types of accounts.
Add, change, and delete system login for workstation access for operators/users.
Schedule and automatically execute reports and commands through an events calendar that signals system to automatically perform the action at a specified date and time.
Specify system time periods (such as Breakfast, Lunch, Dinner, etc.) for use in accounting and reporting.
Perform system backups automatically and on demand.
Provide user definable configurations for reader locations and meal/debit/credit plans which can be done from any workstation, without requiring software reprogramming from the Bidder.
System will monitor the status of card readers at each location (online, off-line)
System security features must include:
Track account creation and last modification by user name/time/location.
Record Workstation modifications to cardholder accounts as transactions.
Automatically uploads off-line transactions.
Incorporates cardholder account balance protection when a card is lost.

General System Software must provide:
Ability to use both SSN and ISO numbers for each cardholder, while using only one base account for each cardholder
A means to add, change, and delete cardholder accounts individually or by range of accounts with a common identifier field
Operation of transaction processing for all-campus debit and credit card activity:
Log cardholder account transactions (deposits, adjustments, sales)
Copier reader application
On-line copier control, operating in conjunction with the campus card transaction processing system
Reporting for each copy machine reader location

Vending reader application:
On-line vending control, operating in conjunction with the campus card transaction processing system
Reporting for each vending machine reader location.
Door Access application:
Multiple access times and locations for each cardholder
Access set-up to include days of week, time range, multiple location ranges
Tracking and reporting on where, when, who, denied and door ajar
On-line, real time workstation deactivation of access for cardholder or reader location.

4.   Multiple, user programmable plans/privileges for meals, debit and credit points, door access, and activity verification per cardholder record
Meal/Point plans that allow price defaults and discounts at certain locations
Ability to reset balances automatically by day, week, time/meal period
User-programmable counters (independent of account balance) on each cardholder account that increment transaction amounts for any plan, as well as a global counter that increments all transaction amounts in all plans for each cardholder account.
Demographic information (name, multiple addresses, memo fields)
A way to get messages to cardholders over the system. Please describe.
On-line, real-time transaction updates/changes, so that cardholder accounts and transaction reports reflect the changes immediately
Provide user-defined data fields for privilege verification at different campus locations i.e., allowing use of athletic events, recreational centers, services in campus departments, etc.
Please indicate how many of these data fields are possible for each cardholder account
Provide for 24-hour unattended operation of system transaction processing and report running

Reporting Software:
Include a sample of each report that resides on your system. The reporting software must provide:
Reports can be user-scheduled to run automatically (without operator attention) for pre-set days and times
Report output to printer, console or file
Reporting of workstation transactions for a specified workstation location or user/operator for a specified range of dates and times.
Reports showing current balance in each cardholder account for specific meal or debit plans
Usage reports showing total head count and sales for each location, broken down by meal or debit plan, for a user-defined date or time range (daily, weekly, monthly)
Reconciliation of the balances of credit/debit accounts with the totals of all reader transactions for a specified date
Reports showing lists and totals of those cardholders entering an activity or facility, by location and for user-specified dates/times
Door access reports, by location, time, date-showing which cardholders were permitted entry

6.   SYSTEM WARRANTY
        The proposed System must be covered by a 365-day warranty from the date the system acceptance test is completed and accepted. During this period, any defects in the system will be corrected at no additional charge as described below:

Failed card readers to be sent to Bidder for repair. Maximum turnaround time must be 10 days.
Failed computer system components will be replaced at no charge and delivered within 24 hours of the reported failure.
Failure of the entire computer system or any software to meet the requirements of this RFP will be corrected at no charge during the warranty period. This includes any necessary software modifications.

7.   SYSTEM MAINTENANCE AND SUPPORT

An ongoing annual service maintenance agreement must be provided. This agreement must cover all System hardware and software.

Updates and enhancements to the system software must be provided at no additional cost to Oregon State University.

A minimum of one year continued service and support must be provided for old software releases when software upgrades are purchased by Oregon State University.

The on-line transaction processor is to be considered high-priority, and the service maintenance agreement must provide that, when defective, a loaner part will be delivered within 24 hours of the reported failure.

The Bidder must provide Oregon State University with System implementation and installation support and assistance. A description may be included under the Desirable Features Section.

The System must be delivered and installed on campus as follows:

June 15, 1998   2,500 Printed DuoProx ID card blanks delivered.

July 15, 1998   Complete system hardware, software and card readers delivered.

     August 15, 1998   Installed and operational:
Complete System hardware, software, and card readers

     August 25, 1998   Initial operator training completed.

     September 15, 1998 Acceptance Test Completed

8. ACCEPTANCE TEST

Before final acceptance, the System must be demonstrated to meet all of the performance, installation, and training specifications in this document, to the satisfaction of the Oregon State University representatives. Successful completion of the following tests constitutes acceptable performance:

Continuous Operation Test - Each card reader, and the on-line transaction processor must operate under normal load conditions for a 30-day period.

Power Failure Test - Each card reader must pass a simulated AC power failure test. When power is restored, each reader must power up and return to online status. Stored transactions must be automatically uploaded to the CPU.

The on-line transaction processor must pass a simulated AC power failure test. During this period, the system must function normally with all card readers online while the system runs on backup power. Neither the removal nor the restoration of AC power may result in any loss of data.

Communications Failure Test - Each card reader must pass a simulated communications failure test (i.e., interrupted communications between the card reader and the on-line transaction processor). All devices must continue to function normally and store transactions. When communications are restored, the card readers must automatically upload stored transactions to the on-line transaction processor.

Backup Test - The CPU must perform a full backup once a day for a consecutive 14-day period.

Download/Upload Test - The on-line transaction processor must be able to download or merge data from a remote computer, and upload data to a remote computer.

The system will not be considered acceptable if:

Any transactions are lost or data integrity is destroyed.

Any card reader fails to transition from online to off-line operation, and vice versa.

The reader validation response time exceeds 2 seconds.

DESIRABLE FEATURES   Maximum Points:

Possible Points

1. ID CARD SPECIFICATION: 10
HID Multiple Technology Proximity (DuoProx) as secondary card stock,
including all features of standard card stock listed under Mandatory
Requirements, Section 1.

HARDWARE
SNMP ability 10
Hardware supported RAID (level 1 or 5), duplexed drives 10
The modem for remote diagnostics communicates directly through the
server 5
Optical drive for system back-up 10
Windows NT Server 20

3. CARD READERS
Please provide a diagram detailing your System's typical communication
topology between the transaction processor and readers/workstations. 10
Please specifically detail how the copier reader communicates with the
on-line transaction processor. 5
Please list which of your card reader models can communicate with the
transaction processor across the campus network. 5
Please describe how each of your reader models indicate an off-line
condition. 5
Please complete and return the attached Card Reader/Peripheral Equipment
worksheet 180
f.   Door Access:
Bidder will provide HID proximity readers which communicate with
the transaction processor. 10
Please describe how your access reader control electronics can be
mounted, i.e., (maximum distance from reader, behind a wall, etc.) 5
Please describe how your door access readers provide off-line
authorization for access. 5
Door Access application and readers allow key override. 5
Door Access readers support an optional PIN pad 5
OSU will install door hardware, bidder will install connections to
readers. 5
Door Access readers and recommended hardware are compatible with
Best or Schlage commercial grade lock mechanisms. 5
Point-of-Sale (POS) Readers:
Full-featured POS readers can report PLU key totals for given date
Ranges 5
h.   Vending Readers:
Describe any tamper-resistant qualities of your vending readers. 5
Describe how your vending readers operate during system
back-up. 5
Describe how your Remote Value Add-On terminal cabinet is
tamper resistant, and whether it includes a monitor or alarm to protect
deposits. 10
Portable Card Readers:
Holds a database of a minimum of 2500 accounts for activity privilege
verification and meal plan or debit/credit plan transactions 5
Uploads transactions automatically upon connection to the on-line
transaction processor 5

4. SOFTWARE

a.   Describe in general how your software for managing ID card accounts is structured. Define how your software uses privilege verification, meal and point/dollar plan operations, and how the features interact with card reader locations.   10
b.   Provide a copy of your system's user manual.   10
c.   Provide a description of your next anticipated major system upgrade and date of release. Please include what the cost to OSU would be to upgrade from your current proposed system to the next, upgraded system. (i.e., what, when, and how much)?   20
Provide a copy of your cardholder account (screen), showing all information fields.   10
Describe how your system platform and readers will handle the Year 2000 transition.   20
Describe how your company will assist OSU in converting all current and backup account and transaction data of the current OSU campus system, to your system's format.   20
Workstation Software:
32 bit application that runs in Windows   20
When running transaction or other reports, how does your workstation software search the database? (by account number, name, other fields)   5
Bidder will provide OSU representative with access to a working System for testing   10

System Administration Software:
1.   Ability for system administrator to terminate any workstation session from a workstation or server console   5
System administrator can grant or deny access for each user to specific debit/credit plans and privileges/activities   10
System Administrator can grant a user the ability to open new accounts, but deny the ability to close accounts on the system   10
System Administrator can assign operators to
        specific CRTs.   5
Provide a copy of your Password/login set-up screen.   10
Events calendar or time scheduler automatically runs reports or commands either hourly, daily, weekly, monthly, annually, or on a specific date/time.   20

General System Software Features:
Describe the Database Management System   30
The system sounds an audible signal at workstation or server console when card readers go off-line.   5
Transaction processing for all-campus debit and credit card activity includes:
a. Minimum 100 different meal/debit/credit plan choices system-wide   10
system has Smart Search so different plans of cardholders can be used at different reader locations.   10
Transactions post to cardholder accounts and may be viewed immediately.   10
Please describe how your system software processes card transactions during system backup.   10
d.   Describe how your system software processes card transactions during system backup.   10

Reporting Software features:
Describe how your system software accesses previous transaction

history, both online and through archives, including the time it would take a workstation to access a transaction which occurred 6 months prior, and how a transaction report can be run for the past month, 6 months ago, and 1 year ago. 10

User created custom report writer using SQL structure 20

Option to suppress ID# on reports 5

Reports showing various system configurations (i.e. set up of debit plans, locations, communications) 5

Instant display or printing of transaction lists via Workstation for a cardholder, a reader location, or a specific meal/debit plan 10

Reports of both dining and activity (privilege verification) location usage, by time intervals (i.e., totals of head count and sales for every 15 minutes, 30 minutes, hour, etc.) 5

Report of Point of Sale reader transactions, by individual operators (clerks) for user-specified dates/times 5

Journal reports of Point of Sale reader location transactions from a PC workstation for specified dates 5

Cardholder account demographic reports, by selected demographic fields (i.e., all female students with last name of Taylor) 5

5. DIGITAL IMAGING CARD PRODUCTION SYSTEM:

a.   Bidder shall describe the Digital Imaging system, its components and features, either in text or with printed material. 20

    b.   32 bit application that runs in Windows 20

c.   Relational database management system which includes the capability of user-defined report generation 10

    d.   Prints 3 of 9 bar code, number generation linked through digital card design on software. 10

e.   Capability for custom design including, fields for photograph, name, I.D.#, at least 2 status descriptors. 10

f.   Digital Imaging System printer hardware includes an encoder which will encode the ID number on the magnetic stripe of the card during printing. 10

6. SYSTEM MAINTENANCE & SUPPORT:

Fully describe the annual maintenance agreement and coverage for your proposed system and readers. (Include costs for this maintenance agreement from year 2 through 5). 20

Fully describe the system installation and implementation support services that will be provided. (Include the associated costs for these services in the Financial Proposal section). 20

Fully describe your system administrator and operator training programs for hardware and software. (Include the associated costs for these services in the Financial Proposal section). 20

Fully describe your Customer Service and Support program. Include your company's procedures for customers to follow for system and reader software, system hardware, and card reader problems. (Include any associated costs for Customer Service in the Financial Proposal section). 20

At the option of Oregon State University, bidder must be willing to participate in a disaster recovery plan by agreeing to make available all hardware and software on a temporary, as-needed basis. Fully describe this program. 10

Bidder provides a toll-free service telephone number (24 hours a day, seven days a week). 10

7. INTERFACE TO EXISTING SYSTEMS

Bidder shall describe their interface of the transaction processing system with
the following third-party systems:

DataCard (QuikWorks) Digital Imaging System	25	
Fastec Point-of-Sale Systems/Equipment		30
Library Systems (Oasis)	20	
Novell print queues for metering printing	30	

8. SYSTEM USER GROUP

Fully explain if there is an established System user group, what part the user
group plays in System development, and how often the user group meets.　　20

9. BIDDER REFERENCES

Bidder shall demonstrate an established, successful track record of past
performance in providing products and service closely related to the
requirements specified in this RFP.　　20

Proposals must include four reference accounts/installations, showing company
experience in receiving contracts for the delivery of campus card systems
similar to the one proposed, to other college and/or university clients. The
reference accounts must be using the Bidder's proposed System as the primary
campus card management system.

Information should include the college/university name, address, telephone
number, and the name and title of the person to contact.

Two of the installations shall have been completed in the last 18 months; the
remaining two installations shall have been completed three or more years ago.

At the University's option, the University, prior to award will be contacting the references.
Professional reference contacts shall be the Contract Administrator or person primarily
responsible for oversight of any contract or agreement with the bidder that supplies the bid brand
product line. Information provided shall include: Name and Address of the Client; Phone
Number; Contact Person and Title; Scope of Contract(s) held.

The references contacted will be asked to rate the bidder, for each question, on a scale of 1 to 5
(5 being best).

The general categories of questions to be asked are:

Quality of customer service, professionalism, etc.

Quality and Effectiveness of Training

Preventative Maintenance Program

Installation and Removal of equipment

Suitability of Equipment to customer needs

Equipment Performance over time Compared to when New

Responsiveness to Service Calls

Vendor's ability to take on new business

Vendor Performance as per agreement

Overall Customer Satisfaction with Vendor

The reference check will be used as one of the tests of responsibility. Should the apparent successful bidder, or subsequent apparent successful bidder upon any rejections, obtain an average total score of less than 30 points, or score Ones (1's) or Zeros (0's) on a total of five questions from all vendors (combined), that bidder will be determined non responsible for purposes of award and shall be rejected.

The University shall attempt to contact any references provided a maximum of three (3) times. If after three attempts, the references provided are unable to be contacted, the bidder shall receive zero (0) points for all questions for that reference. If more than three (3) references are provided, the State shall evaluate only the first three (3) reference responses received.

Please note that the above does not limit the University in its test of responsibility. The University reserves the right to utilize other resources to determine a bidder's responsibility.

INVESTIGATION OF REFERENCES: The University reserves the right to investigate the references and the past performance of any bidder with respect to its successful performance of similar projects, compliance with specifications and contractual obligations, its completion or delivery of a project on schedule, and its lawful payment of suppliers, subcontractors, and workers. OSU may postpone the award or execution of the contract after the announcement of the apparent successful bidder in order to complete its investigation. The University reserves its right to reject any bid response or to reject all bid responses at any time prior to the issuance of a "Notice to Proceed."

ADDITIONAL INFORMATION REQUIRED FROM VENDORS: Bidders must respond to each mandatory requirement listed in the "SPECIFICATIONS AND REQUIREMENTS" section. In addition to the responses to the mandatories, bidder's must provide responses to each item below:

What are OSU's responsibilities for site preparation information, power, environmental, floor space, and customer supplied cabinetry?

What other services and/or equipment would we have to obtain that is not supplied by your company?

Recommend make and model of modems and number of telephone or communications lines for each site.

What are the user responsibilities for maintenance? What supplies are needed to carry out these responsibilities? Which of those supplies are available from the vendor? What is the cost of the supplies?

****

PROPOSER'S FORMS: Any additional documents that the proposer submits to OSU must not conflict with the intent or terms and conditions of the RFP, and therefore, must be submitted with the bid. Examples of these forms are:

Maintenance agreements (hardware or software)
Licensing agreements

FINANCIAL PROPOSAL PREPARATION INSTRUCTIONS

Bidders' financial proposals must include all information needed for OSU to determine the total system cost to OSU. OSU will consider all information submitted by the proposer and known by OSU when determining the total system cost.

Provide the cost of the complete system with all transaction processing system hardware (50,000 cardholders, 130 reader locations), all software, and the following applications included in the price. Please also list incremental prices for each of the applications below as if they were to be added to the system after the initial installation:
Door Access Application
Vending Application
Copier Application
Digital Imaging Card Production Application and Equipment (2 Image Capture stations and printers).
System capacity and software for 20 remote PC workstations.

All card reader and encoder prices to be listed separate from the base system. Prices will be based on the following approximate numbers of readers:

Privilege Verification Readers	9	POS/Limited Features	31
Journal/Receipt Printers	20	POS/Full-Featured	10
Cash Drawers	8	Customer Display	22
Proximity Access Readers	40	Kitchen Monitors	2
Copier Readers	30	ABA Access Readers	2

The breakdown of buildings in which card readers are housed is as follows:
McNary Res. Hall Dining   2 Full POS, 6 Limited POS
       Arnold Deli & Store   3 Full POS
       West Res. Hall Dining   3 Full POS, 6 Limited POS
       Memorial Union 2 Full POS, 11 Limited POS
Library 30 Copier, 1 Limited POS, 1 Remote Value Add-on terminal
Dixon Rec. Ctr/Outdoor Ctr./Langton   2 Limited POS, 3 Privilege Verif. (Adjacent buildings)
Gilbert Addition 3 Limited POS
Climbing Center & Gill Coliseum 4 Privilege Verification, (Adjacent buildings)
Future locations unknown   2 Limited POS, 2 Privilege Verification
       Residence Halls (2 at each)   40 Proximity Door Access Readers
       Snell Hall   2 ABA Door Access Readers

Card stock (10,000) with pre-printed, 4-color process, 1 color drop-in front, and ABA magnetic stripe.

Card stock (2,500) with all of the above features, plus HID Proximity.

System Interface costs for the following applications:
DataCard (Quikworks) Digital Imaging System
Fastec Point-of-Sale Systems/Equipment
Library Systems (Oasis)
Novell print queues for metering lazer printers

System Installation and Implementation charges:

System Administrator and Operator Training Charges:

Customer Service costs outside of those covered under the annual maintenance agreement:

FINANCIAL PROPOSAL EVALUATION AND POINTS AWARD METHODOLOGY

The financial proposals will be awarded points based on the lowest total cost of the proposed system to OSU. The total number of price points available will be 1200.

Bidders price proposals must conform to the mandatory requirements governing the design and requirements of the system. In addition, bidders price proposal must include all features, characteristics and functions included as proposal response for award of desirable points.

The bidder who proposes the system with the lowest total cost to OSU will receive the maximum amount of price points (1200 points). Bidders whose system total cost is higher than the lowest will receive a fewer number of price points in a relational manner as described below.

Example:

Bidder A's system cost is found to be $275.00 (the lowest).
    Bidder A is awarded 1200 Price Points
Bidder B's system cost total is found to be $302.00
    Bidder B is awarded 1092 Price Points (275/302 X 1200)
Bidder C's system cost total is found to be $351.00
    Bidder C is awarded 940 Price Points (275/351 X 1200)
Bidder D's system cost total is found to be $388.00
    Bidder D is awarded 850 Price Points (275/388 X 1200)

PART VI - BIDDER CERTIFICATIONS

EACH BIDDER (PROPOSER) MUST READ AND COMPLY WITH THE FOLLOWING SECTIONS. FAILURE TO DO SO MAY RESULT IN BID (PROPOSAL) REJECTION.

SECTION I: RESIDENCY INFORMATION

ORS 279.029 (2) states "In determining the lowest responsible bidder, a public contracting agency shall, for the purpose of awarding the contract, add a percent increase on the bid of a nonresident bidder equal to the percent, if any, of the preference given to that bidder in the state in which the bidder resides."

"Resident bidder" means a bidder that has paid unemployment taxes or income taxes in this state during the 12 calendar months immediately preceding submission of the bid, has a business address in this state and has stated in the bid whether the bidder is a "resident bidder". (ORS 279.029(6) (b))

"Non-resident bidder" means a bidder who is not a "resident bidder" as defined above. (ORS 279.029(6) (c))

    a. Check one: Bidder is a ( ) resident bidder ( ) non-resident bidder.

    b. If a resident bidder, enter your Oregon business address:

    _____

    _____

    c. If a non-resident bidder, enter state of residency: _____

d. If a non-resident bidder, do you or your firm receive, or are you or your firm eligible for, any preference in award of contracts with your state's government or with other governmental bodies in your state? Check one: ( ) Yes ( ) No
If yes: state the preference percentage: _____%
If yes, but not a percentage of bid price, describe the preference:

_____
If yes, state the law or regulation that allows the preference described
(legal citation): _____

SECTION II : CERTIFICATION OF COMPLIANCE WITH TAX LAWS

I, the undersigned duly authorized representative of the bidder (proposer), hereby certify that the bidder (proposer) is not, to the best of my knowledge, in violation of any Oregon tax law. For purpose of this certification, "Oregon Tax Laws" are ORS Chapters 118, 119, 314, 316, 317, 318, 320, 321 and 323, and Sections 10 to 20, Chapter 533, Oregon Laws 1981 as amended by Chapter 16, Oregon Laws 1982 (Special Session); the Homeowners and Renters Property Tax Relief Program under ORS 310.630 to 310.690; and any local tax laws administered by the Oregon Department of Revenue under ORS 305.620.

SECTION III: FINANCIAL RESPONSIBILITY

OSU reserves the right, pursuant to OAR 125-30-003, to investigate and evaluate, at any time prior to award and execution of the contract, the lowest responsible bidder's/apparent successful proposer's financial responsibility to perform the contract. Submission of a signed bid/proposal shall constitute approval for OSU to obtain any credit report information OSU deems necessary to conduct the evaluation. OSU shall notify the lowest responsible bidder/apparent successful proposer, in writing, of any other documentation required, which may include, but need not be limited to, recent profit-and-loss history; current balance statements; assets-to-liabilities ratio, including number and amount of secured versus unsecured creditor claims; availability of short and long-term financing; bonding capacity and credit information, etc. Failure to promptly provide this information shall result in bid/proposal rejection.

OSU may postpone the award or execution of the contract after announcement of the lowest responsible bidder/apparent successful proposer in order to complete its investigation and evaluation. Failure of the lowest bidder/apparent successful proposer to demonstrate financial responsibility, as required under OAR 125-30-003, shall render the bidder/proposer nonresponsible and shall constitute grounds for bid/proposal rejection, as required under OAR 137-30-100.

SIGNATURE BLOCK

SIGNATURE OF BIDDER'S DULY AUTHORIZED REPRESENTATIVE FOR
THIS PROPOSAL MUST BE SIGNED IN INK BY AN AUTHORIZED REPRESENTATIVE OF THE BIDDER; ANY ALTERATIONS OR ERASURES TO THE PROPOSAL MUST BE INITIALED IN INK BY THE UNDERSIGNED AUTHORIZED REPRESENTATIVE.

The undersigned agrees and certifies that he/she:

1. Has read and understands all bid (proposal) instructions, specifications, and terms and conditions contained herein (including the attachments listed in this document);

2. Is an authorized representative of the bidder, that the information provided in this proposal is true and accurate, and that providing incorrect or incomplete information may be cause for bid rejection or contract termination;

3. Is bound by and will comply with all requirements, specifications, and terms and conditions contained herein; and

4. Will furnish the designated item (s) and/or service(s) in accordance with the bid and the contract.

5. BIDDER WILL PROVIDE/FURNISH FEDERAL EMPLOYEE IDENTIFICATION NUMBER OR SOCIAL SECURITY NUMBER WITH PROPOSAL SUBMISSION.

Authorized Signature: _____

Title: _____

FEIN ID# or SSN# (required) _____

Contact Person (Type or Print): _____

Telephone Number: (___) _____   Fax Number: (___) _____

UPON COMPLETION OF RFP EVALUATION, OSU WILL ISSUE A CONTRACT DOCUMENT THAT WILL BE SIGNED BY ALL PARTIES.

PAGE 37

PAGE 27

Office of Business Services (Purchasing
Oregon State University
644 SW 13th Street
Corvallis, Oregon 97333-4238
Telephone: 541-737-4261   Fax: 541-737-2170

VENDORS

ACCESS GLOBAL FINANCIAL CORPORATION
318 West Adams. Ste. 1500
Chicago, IL 60606
Contact: Robert DaiSanto, President
Tel: (312) 641-6340
Fax: (312) 641-3536
E-mail: rjaisanto@accessglobal.net

ACTIVECARD
6531 Dumbarton Circle
Fremont, CA 94555
Contact: Rodman Dtuhlmuller
Direct: (510) 574-1733
Mobil: (408) 497-4643
Tel: (510) 574-0100
Fax: (510) 574-0101
E-mail: rstuhlmuller@activcard.com
Web: www.activcard.com

ADVANCED CARD TECHNOLOGY OF CANADA
831 Miriam Road
Pickering, ON, Canada l1W 1X7
Contact: Catherine Johnson
President & CEO
Tel: 905-420-3520
Fax: 905-420-2729
E-mail: info@actcda.com

ALLSAFE COMPANY, INC.
P.O. Box 825
Buffalo, NY 14240
Contact: James E. Pokornowski, President
Tel: (716) 896-4241
E-mail: jpokomowski@allsafe.com

AMERICAN TERMINAL EXCHANGE INC.
POS Terminal Services
Commerce Park, 5 Corporate Dr.
Danbury, CT 06810-4310
Contact: Joseph Dillulio, President
Tel: (203) 830-4848
Fax: (203) 830-4859

AMERIPLAST
Printers
3041 West McNab Road
Pompano Beach, FL 33069 USA
Tel: (954) 984-4818
Fax: (954) 984-4818
E- mail: leosmith@ameriplast.com
Web: www.ameriplast.com

APPLIED CARD SYSTEMS
POS Terminal Services
2 Read's Way
New Castle, DE 19720
Contact: Rocco A. Abessinio, President
Tel: (302) 322-9111
Fax: (302) 322-9122

ARAMARK CORPORATION
7099 Cove Creek Dr.
Sherrils Ford, NC 28673
Contact: Judith Carter, Systems Supervisor
PHONE: 704-483-7148
E-mail: Carter-judy@aramark.com

ARIA WIRELESS SYSTEMS, INC.
Communication equipment manufacturer
Serving international EFT Market
140 Mid Country Dr.
Orchard Park, NY 14127
Contact: Frank J. Perpiglin, Chairman and CEO
Tel: (716) 662-0874
Fax: (716) 662-1589

ASK! TECHNICAL GROUP INC.
POS Terminal Services
4580 Biedler Rd.
Willoughby, OH 44094
Contact: John P. McCarthy, Vice President
Tel: (216) 951-2880
Fax: (216) 951-2818

ATALLA CORPORATION, A TANDEM COMPANY
Design and manufactures point-of-sale payment-acceptance terminals
2304 Zanker Rd.
San Jose, CA 95131
Contact: Bob Gargus, President
Tel: (408) 435-8850
Fax: (408) 435-8850

ATS TELEPHONE & DATA SYSTEMS
POS Terminal Services
3955 Vantech Dr., Suite 7
Memphis, TN 38115
Contact: Mack Crowder, President
Tel: (901) 797-3000
Fax: (901) 797-2829

AT&T CAMPUSWIDE ACCESS SOLUTIONS
Development of software & hardware products
2362 W. Shangri-La Rd.
Phoenix, AX 85026
Contact: Lowell Adkins, Vice President
PHONE: 800-528-0465
www.campuswide.com

ATLANTEK, INC.
Supplier of Products and Technology in Electronic Image Printing, Direct Plastic Card Printing, Medical Recording, Bar Code Printing
10 High St.
Wakefield, RI 02879
Contact: Christine DenBleyker, Sales
Tel: (401) 783-5700
Fax: (401) 783-9881

AURORA MERCHANT SYSTEMS
POS Termianl Services
1860 Sierra Gardens
Roseville, CA 95661
Contact: Richard Graves, President
Tel: (916) 773-8331
Fax: (916) 773-1751

BADGINGSOLUTIONS.COM
2486 Atlanta Road
Smyrna, GA 30080
Contact: Earl Brewington, Jr., President
Tel: 800-228-6522
Fax: 770-432-2753

BENCHMARK TECHNOLOGIES INC.
POS Terminal Services
2636 Walnut Hill Ln. Suite 350
Dallas, TX 75229
Contact: Ken Shepherd, President
Tel: (214) 352-1100
Fax: (214) 352-1185

BEST ACESS SYSTEM
6161 East 75th Street
Indianapolis, IN 46250
Contact: Jena Lasch
Tel: (317) 849-2255 x 2354
Fax: (317) 596-4810
E-mail: laschj@bestlook.com

BUIL INFORMATION SYSTEMS
300 Concord Rd. MS849A
Billerica, MA 01821-4186
Contact: Christopher Martin
Tel: (978) 294-3668
Fax: (978) 294-3671
E-mail: christoper.martin@buil.com

CAMPUS CARD SYSTEMS, A DIVISION OF ICOLLEGE, INC.
770 22nd Avenue, South
Brookings, SD 57006
Contact: Sherryl Wieczorek
Tel: 605-694-6311
E-mail: wieczorek@icollege.com

CBORD GROUP, INC
Card Systems
61 Brown Road
Ithaca, NY 14850
Tel: (607) 257-2410
Web: www.cbord.com/odyssey

CEI-COLLEGE ENTERPRISES INC.
Card Systems, Publishing, Copyright Services Printing
21201 Victory Blvd., Ste 270
Canoga Park. CA 91303
Contact: Greg Baker, Vice President for CEI Card Systems
Tel: 818-615-0560

CHERRY ELECTRICAL PRODUCTS
Biometrics
3600 Sunset Ave.
Waukegan, IL 50087
Contact: Mike Harvey, Keyboard Marketing
Manager
Tel: (847) 360-3379
Fax: (847) 360-3414
E-mail: mharvey@cherrycorp.com

CITIBANK e-CITI
*e-Citi on campus, ID Card Systems Integration,
Intranet Solutions, Free Internet Banking Service
Free, unlimited Citibank ATM access, Campus
Banking Centers, Marketing Smart Cards,
Financial Services for Colleges and Universities*
8430 W. Bryn Mawr
Chicago, IL 60631
Contact: Gil Ruman, Business Development
e-Citi on Campus
PHONE: 773-380-5601
E-mail: gil.ruman@citicorp.com
www.ecitioncampus.com

CITIZEN CBM AMERICA CORP.
POS Terminal Service
Two Executive Dr., Suite 645
Contact: Jeffrey Lee Scott, Eastern Regional
Coordinator
Tel: (201) 944-1313
Fax: (201) 944-6669

COINMACH LAUNDRY
8 Corporate Drive
Cranbury, NJ 08512
Contact:Ryan Donnelly, Dir. of Collegiate
Services
Tel: 800-232-9274
Fax: 609-395-6797
E-mail: cls@coinmachcorp.com

COLLEGIATE CONCEPTS
Card Accessory
4276 Colleen Circle
Arden Hills, MN 55112
Contact: Jon Van Buren, Owner
Tel: 888-438-9268
Fax: 651-638-2221
E-mail: imprint@uswest.net

COLOR ID
2480 Chartwell Center Dr., Suite F
Cornelius, NC 28031 USA
Contact: Dan Smith
Tel: (704) 987-2231
Fax: (704) 987-2240
E-mail: dsmith@colorid.com

COMDATA NETWORK INC.
POS Terminal services
5301 Maryland Way
Brentwood, TN 37017
Contact: George McTavish, CEO
Tel: (615) 370-7500
Fax: (615) 370-7560

CONTINENTAL PLASTIC CARD COMPANY
Card Security System
3651 NW 120th Ave
Coral Springs, FL 33065
Tel: (954) 753-0670
Fax: (954) 341-3479
E-mail: info@continentalplasticcard.com
Web: www.continentalplasticcard.com

COMMERCE BANK
Card banking
811 Main St.
P.O. Box 13607
Kansas City, MO 64199-3607
Contact: Andrew Briscoe
University Card Coordinator
Tel: 816-760-8178
www.commercebank.com

CREDENTIA DATACARD GROUP
11111 Bren Road West
Minneapolis, MN 55343
Contact: John Orton, President
Tel: (612) 988-1571
Fax: (612) 988-2658
E-mail: jon_orton@datacard.com

CREDIT CARD SYSTEMS INC.
POS Terminal Services
180 Shepard Ave.
Wheeling, IL 60090
Contact: Peter Lazzari, President
Tel: (800) 747-1269
Fax: (708) 459-1296

CYBERMARK
Card System Integrator
Smart Card Solutions
11600 Sunrise Valley Drive
Suite 400
Reston, VA 20191-1412
Contact: VP, Marketing
Tel: 703-7588710
www.cybermark.com

DATACAP SYSTEM, INC.
Manufactures of Datacaptor 2000
series ECR/POS terminals
212A Progress Dr.
Montgomeryville, PA 55440
Contact: Gale Peters, VP of Marketing and Sales
Tel: (215) 699-7051
Fax: (215) 699-6779

DATACARD GROUP
Durable, multipurpose student Ids, Photo ID
Systems with bar code, magnetic stripe, and smart
card capabilities, All-in-one Campus Cards
11111 Bren Rd., Suite 159
Chattanooga, TN 37421
Contact: Glenn Highland, President and CEO
Tel: (800) 621-6972 ext. 218
1-877-273-3368, ext. 6537
Fax: (612) 931-0418
www.datacard.com

DATASTRIP, INC.
Provider of secure high-density 2D barcode
software and hardware, and biometric
verification devices.
502 West 13th St.
Austin, TX 78701
Contact: Joseph Cipriano
Tel: 512-477-7277
www.datastrip.com

DEBITEK, INC.
Auditing, chip and off-line vending
2115 Chapman Road, Suite 159
Chattanooga, TN 37421
Contact: Ron Farmer, Chief Operating Officer
Tel: (423) 894-6177
Fax: (423) 855-7554
E-mail: sales@debitek.com
Web: www.debitek.com

DIEBOLD, INC.
Providing funds settlement and collection
5995 Mayfair Rd.
North Canton, OH 44720
Contact: Robert W. Mahoney, Chairman of
the Board, CEO and President
Tel: (330) 490-6262
Tel: (800) 999-3600

DIRECT DATA INC.
Manufactures and distributes transaction termi-
nals and peripherals for payment systems
810 Cardinal Ln
Hartland, WI 55029
Contact: Richard P. Draper, Chairman
Tel: (414) 367-5120
Fax: (414) 367-3637

DREAM DESIGNS
Graphic Designs
2508 W. Davis Suite 202
Conroe, TX 77304
Tel: (936) 441-5288
Fax: (936) 756-2402
E-mail: mlopez@dreamdesigns.com
Web: www.dreamdesigns.com

DREIFUS ASSOCIATES, LTD.
Smart Card Consulting
Systems Integration
801 W. State Rd. 436, Suite 2035
Altamonte Springs, FL 32714
Contact: Andrew Stuart, Consultant
Tel: (407) 855-5477
Fax: (407) 865-5478
E-mail: andrew.stuart@dreifus.com

DRESSER INDUSTRIES INC.
Wayne dispenser card processing terminal printer
and pin pad
124 W. College Ave.
Salisbury, MD 21801
Contact: John P. Ryan, Vice President of
Sales and Marketing
Tel: (410) 546-6600
Fax: (410) 546-6882

DUPONT TEIJIN FILMS
Bermuda Hundred
Hopewell, VA 23860
Contact: Simon Shepherd
Technical Services Engineering
Tel: 804-530-4042
Fax: 804-530-9862
E-mail: simon.j.shepherd@usa.dupont.co

DYNCOM
1317 LaPorte Ave.
Ft. Collins, CO 80521
Contact: David Breeding, Development Manager
Tel: 970-416-0001
E-mail: Dabr@d-c.com

E.I. DUPONT DE NEMOURS & CO.
DuPont Polyester Films
High Performance Cards
P.O.Box 411
Hopewell, VA 23860
Contact: Bill Deep, Market Development
Manager, North and South America
Tel: (804) 530-9365
Fax: (804) 530-9862
E-mail: bill.w.deep@usa.dupont.com

ELECTRONIC DATA MAGNETICS
Smart Card, Magnetic Stripe MFG. & Issuers
1492 Mountain Reserve Drive
Kennesaw, GA 30152 USA
Tel: (770) 218-0321
Fax: (770) 2180318
Web: www.electronicdata.com

**ELECTRONIC PRINT
COMMUNICATIONS INC.**
Printers
6510 Evenvale Blvd.
Eden Prairie, MN 55344 USA
Tel: (952) 934-5500
Fax: (952) 934-3500
E-mail: epc@mr.net
Web: www.epcconnect.com

ENVOY CORP.
*Maufacturer of FTP. with optional printer; ter-
minal application, software for retail restaurant,
T&-E, fleet, and debit service*
15 Century Blvd., Suite 600
Nashville, TN 37214
Contact: Fred C. Goad, President and CEO
Tel: (615) 885-3700
Fax: (615) 889-9955

FARGO ELECTRONICS, INC.
*Multi-purpose ID Cards, Card Durability, Card
Printers*
6533 Flying Cloud drive
Eden Prarie, MN 55344
Contact: Sharon Steinhoff-Smith
Tel: (800) 459-5636. ext/ 366
Fax: (612) 946-8493
E-mail: ssmith@fargo.com
Web: www.fargo.com

FIRSTAR
5065 Wooster Pike
Cincinnati, OH 45226
Contact: James Marshall, Vice President, Alt
Del-Sales
Tel: 513-979-1330
Fax: 513-979-1355
E-mail: jim_marshall@firstar.com

FUJITSU-ICL SYSTEMS INC.
*Manufacturer of Fujitsu models 7990 and 8770,
A rium 9000 POS line with standard printer*
11085 N. Torrey Pines Rd.
La Jolla , CA 92037
Contact: Rod Powell, President and CEO
Tel: (619) 457-9900
Fax: (619) 457-9982

GASBOY INTERNATIONAL
*Manufacturer of CFN POS system; Check Point
Terminal provides functions of pump control and
ECR*
707 N. Valley Forge Rd.
Landsdale, PA 19446
Contact: Michael Boone, President
Tel: (215) 855-4631
Fax: (215) 855-0341

GB FRANK INTERNATIONAL
POS Terminal Services
3310 Elston Ave.
Chicago, IL 60618
Contact: Scott Robertson, National Sales
Manager
Tel: (312) 463-8500
Fax: (312) 463-6414

GENERAL CREDIT FORMS
POS Terminal Services
3595 Rider Trail South
Earth City, MO 63045
Contact: Joseph McCormick
Tel: (314) 291-8600
Fax: (314) 298-8366

GILBARCO INC.
Fully integrated G-SITR, retail fuel management
console with built-in card reader
7300 W. Friendly Ave.,
P.O.Box 2208
Greensboro, NC 27420
Contact: Mark W. Snowberger, President
Tel: (910) 547-5000
Fax: (910) 292-6871

GEMPLUS
Card management systems, Cryptography, Secu-
rity, Memory and Microprocessor Cards, Smart
Cards, Public Key Smart Cards, Operating
Systems, Personalization, and Training
3 Lagoon Drive, Suite 300
Redwood City, CA 94065
Contact: Marjorie Salembier, Marketing
Manager, Campus Solutions
Tel: (650) 654-2903
marjoriesalembier@gemplus.com
www.gemplus.com

GENERAL METERS CORPORATION
University One-card System, Since 1979,
Designed Card Systems for over 300 College and
University Campuses
1935 Deminion Way
Colorado Springs, CO 80918
Contact: Jeff Zander, Vice President
Tel: 818-591-3575
E-mail: jeffzan@aol.com
www.1card.com

GLEN GOLD, P.A.
Professional Services: Legal/ Patent
11380 Prosperity Farms Road, Suite 209B
Palm Beach Gardens, FL 33410 USA
Tel: (561) 799-6630
Fax: (561) 627-8616
E-mail: patent 1234@aol.com

GODDARD TECHNOLOGY
CORPORATION
Photo ID System
7001-A Pelham Road
Greenville, SC 29615
Contact: Ty Savage, National Sales Manager
Tel: 864-288-1441
Fax: 864-288-1178
E-mail: tysgoddard.com

GRAPHIC VISION DESIGN STUDIO
Graphic Design
5353 North Federal Highway, Suite 209
Fort Lauderdale, Fl 33308
Tel: (954) 492- 0590
Fax: (954) 489-9675
E-mail: graficvision@earthlink.net
Web: www.graphicvision.net

THE HORIZON GROUP INC.
POS Terminal Services
1155 N. Warrson Rd.
St. Louis, MO 63132
Contact: Ken Boody, CEO
Tel: (314) 991-6040
Fax: (314) 991-6041

HYPERCOM INC.
Provides a full range of credit and debit card
POS terminals, PIN pads and card readers,
smart card readers
2851 W. Kathleen Blvd.
Phoenix, AZ 85023
Contact: Albert Irato, President
Tel: (602) 866-5399
Fax: (602) 866-5380

i COLLEGE CAMPUS CARD SYSTEMS
Campus card systems for dining services, vending, Laundry, business machines, activities, and event management.
770 22nd Avenue South
Brookings, SD 57006
Tel: (605) 697-6311
Fax: (605) 697-6304
E-mail: TimAaron@icollege.com

ICMA
P.O.Box 727
Princeton Junction, NJ 08550
Contact: Jeff Bamhardt, Executive Director
Tel: (609) 799-4900
Fax: (609) 799-7032
E-mail: jbamhardt@cmasolutions.com

IDENTICARD SYSTEMS, INC.
P.O. Box 5349
40 Citation Lane
Lancaster,PA 17606-5349
Contact: Gary Funck, Vice president, Marketing
Tel: 717-569-5797, ext. 456
www.identicard.com

IDENTITRONICS
Campus ID System
425 Lively Blvd.
Elk Grove Village, IL 60007
Contact: Robert Herling, General Manager
Tel: (847) 437-2654
Fax: (847) 437-2660
E-mail: gm@identatronics.com

ILCO UNICAN
Integrated campus security solutions, Enhanced access control, Stand-alone locks, On-line access control
Contact: Alicyn Osachuk, Marketing Coordinator
Tel: (514) 735-5410 x 255
1-888-217-5654
Fax: (514) 735-8862
E-mail: commercial.sales@mtl.ilcounican.com
www.ilcounican.com

INTERACTIVE CARDNET TELEPHONE CO.
POS Terminal Services
P.O.Box 15272
Las Vegas, NV 89114
Contact: Stuart Ervin, CEO
Tel: (702) 477-0200
Fax: (702) 385-0033

INTERNATIONAL VERIFACT INC.
Designs, develops, and markets terminals and related products, offering cost-effective, secure eletronics payment processing solution for point-of-sale application
5621 Arapahoe Ave.
Boulder, CO 90303
Contact: George Whitton, Chairman and CEO
Tel: (303) 440-2800
Fax: (303) 442-2438

JAKEWAY COMPANY, INC.
1613 Riverview
Kalamazoo, MI 49004
Contact: Mark Hancock, President
Tel: (616) 383-1250
Fax: (616) 383-1334
E-mail: mhcanes1@aol.com

JSA TECHNOLOGIES, INC.
20 Park Plaza, Suite 482
Boston, MA 02116
Contact: David Johnson, Chief Tech Officer
Tel: 877-572-8324
E-mail: djohnson@jsatech.com

K-VELL CONSULTING
Specializing in technology, organizations build their business, Identifying new services, Marketing, Public Relations
Contact: Kendra Bonnett, President, Marketing
223 Byram Shore Road
Greenwich, CT 06830
Tel: 203-531-6609
Kendra1@ix.netcom.com

LAW OFFICE OF THOMAS K. CROWE
Professional Services: Legal/ Patent
2300 M Street N.W. Suite 800
Washington, D.C. 20037 USA
Tel: (202) 973-2890
Fax: (202) 973-2891
Web: www.tkcrowe.com

LAMINEX
Photo ID System
8350 Arrowridge Blvd.
Charlotte, NC 28273
Contact: Barry Duppstadt
Tel: (704) 679-4170 x 8310
Fax: (704) 679-6453
E-mail: bduppestadt@laminex.com

LIFESTREAM INC.
Links Smart Card privacy and security
Solution with online communication
Contact: Ed Kalin
Tel: (877) 416-9966
Fax: (970) 226-1988
E-mail: ekalin@lifestreamtech.com

LIPMAN USA INC.
Manufacturer of electronic
cash registers and POS products
95 Seaview Blvd. # 200
Port Washington, NY 11050
Contact: Mony Zenou, President
Tel: (516) 484-9895
Fax: (516) 484-9057

LOCKNETICS SECURITY ENGINEERING
575 Birch St.
Forestville, CT 06010
Contact: Michael Higgins, Marketing Mgr.,
Educ. Segment
Tel: (860) 584-9158
Fax: (860) 584-2136

LOGISTICS MANAGEMENT INC.
POS Terminal Services
6269 E. Shelby Dr.
Memphis, TN 38141
Contact: Marty Hashberger, President
Tel: (901) 541-2200
Fax: (901) 541-2222

MAC GRAY SERVICES
22 Water St.
Cambridge, MA 02141
Contact: Robert Looney, V.P. Sales
Tel: (617) 492-4040 x 373
Fax: (617) 868-5357
E-mail: rlooney@macgray

MAC SYSTEMS, INC.
355 Bodwell St., P.O. Box 717
Avon, MA 02322
Contact: Bob McMeninmon
Tel: (508) 599-6112 x 101
Fax: (508) 599-6122
E-mail: mcmenimon@macsystemsinc.com

MARKS USA
5300 New Horizons Blvd.
Amityville, NY 11701
Contact: George Sheppard
Tel: (516) 225-5400 x 27
Fax: (516) 255-6136
E-mail: gsheppard@marksusa.com

MAGTEK
Credit, debit, and stored value, Card Systems,
Emerging Technologies for use in Card Issuing,
Card Acceptance, Cardholder Authentication
480 Sawgrass Corp. Pky., Suite 110
Ft. Lauderdale, FL 33325
Contact: Kiran Gandhi, Vice President
Tel: 954-858-6122
www.magtek.com

MASTERCARD INTERNATIONAL
2000 Purchase St.
Purchase, NY 10577
Contact: Melanie Gluck, Director, U.S. Chip
Team
Tel: (914) 249-1811
Fax: (914) 249-4207
E-mail: melanie_gluck@mastercard.com

MBNA AMERICA
1501 Yamato Rd.
Boca Raton, FL 33431
Contact: Phil Floor, Marketing Floor
Tel: (516) 988-5836
Fax: (516) 988-5845

MCI
Provides telephone service
333 East Osborn Rd., Ste. 200
Phoenix, AZ 85012
Contact: Mr. Alan Bondzio, Senior Manager
Tel: (602) 734-6143
Fax: (602) 734-6130
E-mail: alan.bondzio@wcom.com

MERCHANT SERVICES INC.
POS Terminal Services
One Ames Ct. Suite 105
Plainview, NY 11803
Contact: Ray Sidhom, President
Tel: (516) 576-3344
Fax: (516) 576-3350

MERCHANT SERVICES USA INC.
POS Terminal Services
3917 Westponit Blvd., Suite A
Winston-Salem, NC 27103
Contact: Alex Siafacas, President
Tel: (910) 760-8120
Fax: (910) 760-8134

MICROBILT CORP.
Provides credit card authorization and settlement
devices with signature-capture and embossed
card-reader capabilities
6190 Powers Ferry Rd.
Atlanta, GA 30339
Contact: Dan Corette, Vice President,
Marketing, MicroBilt Payment System
Tel: (404) 955-0313
Fax: (404) 984-5632

MICROSOFT
Smart Cards for Windows
Contact: Mike Dusche, Product Manager of
Smart Cards for Windows
Web: www.microsoft.com/smartcard

MICRO TECHNOLOGY INC.
Provides credit and debit card authorization,
check, guarantee, and inventory control and
customer management
200 Girard St.
Gaithersburg, MD 20877
Contact: Mark Manesh, CEO
Tel: (301) 984-8800
Fax: (301) 984-9125

MISSION FEDERAL CREDIT UNION
5785 Oberlin Dr., Ste 206
San Diego, CA 92121
Contact: Lucy Z. Jones, A.V.P. Card Services
Tel: (619) 546-2078
Fax: (619) 546-9554
E-mail: lucyj@missionfcu.org

MOTOROLA
Provides wireless services
5201 Tollview Dr.
Rolling Meadows, IL 60008
Contact: Lester LaPierre, Sale Manager
Tel: (847) 538-5153
E-mail: flp222@email.mot.com

MONDEX INTERNATIONAL LTD.
47-53 Cannon St.
London, UK EC4M 5SQ
Contact: Peter J. Tilson
Tel: 44171 557 5122
Fax: 44171 557 5322
E-mail: peter.tilson@mondex.com

NATIONAL BANKCARD ASSOCIATION INC.
POS Terminal Services
9089 Clairmont
San Diega, CA 92123
Contact: Glenn Reph, President
Tel: (800) 576-2220
Fax: (619) 576-0613

NATIONAL CITY CORPORATION
225 North Rose
Kalamazoo, MI 49007
Contact: Thomas Ihling, Campus Card
Regional Mgr.
Tel: (616) 376-9033
Fax: (616) 376-7117

NBS TECHNOLOGIES INC.
Specialized POS terminals;
All C language based
POS Division, 5640 Pare
Montreal, Quebec H4P 2M
Contact: Jim Johnson, President
Tel: (514) 735-1341
Fax: (514) 342-9763

NEURON ELECTRONICS INC.
Manufacturer of Magnetic card reader/writers, reader/ write terminals, and hand held CCD bar code scanner
3914 Del Amo Blvd. Suite 902
Torrance, CA 90503
Contact: Steven Stone
Tel: (310) 793-1300
Fax: (310) 793-1304

NORWEST BANK COLORADO N.A.
207 1st Ave.
LaSaile, CO 80645
Contact: Jill Sauter, Location Manager
Tel: (970) 284-5536
Fax: (970) 284-5536

NOVATEK CORP.
POS Terminal Services
3700 N.W. 124th Ave., Suite 137
Coral Springs, FL 33065
Contact: Barry Huffstetler, President
Tel: (305) 341-7700
Fax: (305) 345-9334

NPD & ASSOCIATES
PO Box 589
Newtown Square, PA 19073
Contact: Niles Dally, President
Tel: 610-353-9548
Fax: 610-353-4631
E-mail: ndally@erols.com

NTN INC.
Provides designs ,integrates, markets, and maintains electronic payment systems and specializes in application for multi-line retailers
9 Kane Industrial Dr.
Hudson, MA 01749
Contact: Paul Siegenthaler
Tel: (508) 562-6500
Fax: (508) 562-9681

THE OLIVER ALLEN CORP.
POS Terminal Services
8400 Normandale Lake Blvd., Suite 137
Contact: Charlie Wirth, President
Tel: (612) 832-9400
Fax: (612) 832-9477

ONLINE PIZZA, LLC
101 South 5th St.
Louisville, KY 40202
Contact: Steve Bing
Tel: 502-584-4008
Sbing@prosperitasfund.com

OMRON SYSTEMS INC.
Manufacturer of N>Vision terminal, all with optional printer and PIN pads
55 E. Commerce Dr.
Schaumburg, IL 60173
Contact: Pat Green, President
Tel: (708) 843-0515
Fax: (708) 843-7686

ORANGE COUNTY TEACHER'S
FEDERAL CREDIT UNION
15442 Del Amo Ave.
Tustin, CA 92780
Contact: Jennifer Caruso, Asst. Manager, Card Services
Tel: (714) 258-4000 x 8228
Fax: (714) 258-4217
E-mail: jcaruso@octfcu.org

PACIFIC CASCADE CORP.
POS Terminal Services
1309 N.E. 134th St. Suite E
Contact: Mark A. Curtis, President
Tel: (360) 574-9313
Fax: (360) 574-9325

PENN SECURITY BANK & TRUST CO.
150 N. Washington Ave.
Scranton, PA 18503
Contact: Douglas Duguay, Director, Campus Banking Div.
Tel: 717-346-7741
Fax: (570) 969 –2743
E-mail Dduguay@epix.net

PENNSYLVANIA STATE EMPLOYEES
CREDIT UNION
1 Credit Union Place
Harrisburg, PA 17110
Contact: Denny Beaver, Manager, Campus Card
Tel: 717-777-2059
Fax: 717-720-1121
E-mail: dbeaver@psecu.com

PEREGRIN TECHNOLOGIES INC.
Manufacturer of P300 Scrip dispenser and P700 cast. Dispenser are sold to convenience stores and fast food restaurants and similar retailers
1400 N.W. Compton Dr.
Beaverton, OR 97006
Contact: Sam Bosch
Tel: (503) 690-1111
Fax: (503) 690-1188

PERIPHERAL RESOURCES
POS Terminal Services
9911 Pico Blvd., Suite B-215
Los Angles, CA 90035
Contact: Sue Cheng, CFO
Tel: (800) 533-2297
Fax: (310) 552-2806

PETRO VEND INC.
Manufacturers System2Family of outdoor pay-ment terminal products and PetroPro family of in-store POS family of in-store POS products, featuring the PV3500 fuel Site Controller
6900 Santa Fe Dr.
Hodgkins, IL 60525
Contact: Doug Stewart, President
Tel: (708) 485-4200
Fax: (708) 485-7137

PHOENIX INTERACTIVE VIDEO
Provides instant banking center that combines transaction services with marketing and lead generation for interactive self-service banking
270 Regency Ridge, Suite 210
Centerville, OH 45459
Contact: Kyle MacDonald, Chief Operating Officer
Tel: (513) 439-4511
Fax: (519) 679-6773

PIERCE MAGNETICS
951 Lawson Street
City of Industry, CA 91748
Contact: James Fong, President
Tel: 626-964-9330
Fax: 626-913-0043

PINPOINT RETAIL SYSTEMS INC.
Design, manufactures, sells and supports full line of point-of-sale terminals, POS software, and peripheral products-scanners, printers, customer displays, and built-in credit/debit processing units
30 Fulton Way
Richmond Hills, Ont. L4B 1E6
Contact: Sami Khalife, Chairman
Tel: (905) 731-3314
Fax: (905) 881-6033

PLASTAG CORP.
1800 Greenleaf Ave.
Elk Grove, IL 60007
Contact: Patrick Welch, Director of Marketing
Tel: (847) 258-1000
Fax: (847) 258-1010

PLASTICARD SYSTEM INC.
POS Terminal Services
2917 W. State Rd. 434, Suite 131
Longwood, FL 32779
Contact: Joyce B. Brocker, President
Tel: (407) 869-4120
Fax: (407) 862-1182

PLASTIC GRAPHIC
Graphics
255 Industrial Drive
Wauconda, IL 60084
Tel: (847) 487-2030
Fax: (847) 487-2050
E-mail: bjg1113@aol.com
Web: www.plasticgraphic.com

PNC BANK CORP.
Mail stop F2-F070-22-6
1600 Market Street
Philadelphia, PA 19103-7240
Contact: Joseph Serianni, Vice President
Tel: 215-585-6286
Fax: 215-585-1222
E-mail: joseph.serianni@pncbank.com
www.pnc.com

POS SUPPORT
POS Terminal Services
6414 N.W. 82nd Ave.
Miami, FL 33166
Contact: Rafael Pariente, President
Tel: (305) 552-8165
Fax: (305) 552-8133

PUBLICARD
Smart Card Solutions
1520 Neptune Drive
Boyton, Beach, FL 33426
Contact: Bruce Urquhart, President
Tel: (561) 369-3435
Fax: (561) 369-2623
E-mail: bruce@icardsys.com

QUADAGNO & ASSOCIATES
Card Technology, Payments, Card Technology and Telecommunications, Public Transit, Point-of-Sale Activation Systems
1626 Herron Lane
West Chester, PA 19380
Contact: Peter Quadagno, President
Tel: (610) 344-4860
Fax: (610) 344-2981
E-mail: peterq@quadangno.com

RAM MOBILE DATA
POS Terminal Services
10 Woodbridge Center Dr., Suite 950
Woodbridge, NJ 07095
Contact: William Leneham, President
Tel: (908) 602-5500
Fax: (908) 602-1262

ROBERT HUBER ASSOCIATES
Consultant
Ste. 1072, 13421 N. 43rd Ave.
Phoenix, AZ 85029
Contact: Bob Huber, President
Tel: (602) 439-3118
Fax: (602) 938-1658
E-mail: huber@allcampuscard.com

SAFECOMM, INC.
180 Sheree Boulevard, Suite 3200
Exton, PA 19341
Contact: Dean Deitrich, Marketing Rep
Tel: 610-363-5500, x 103
Fax: 610-363-6055

SCAN TECHNOLOGY, INC.
625-A N.W. 60th St.
Gainsville, Fl 32607
Contact: Stephen Flowers, Director of Marketing
Tel: (352) 332-2093
Fax: (352) 332-7133
E-mail: sflowers@scatec.com
www.scantec.com

SCHLUMBERGER
Card Systems Integration, Planning, Design, Development, and Implementation of Turnkey-integrated Smart Card Solutions
1601 Schlumberger Drive
Moorestown, NJ 08057
Contact: Feryal Allen, National Marketing Manager
Tel: 856-234-8000
Fax: 856-234-7178
E-mail: allen@moorestown.tt.slb.com
www.slb.com/smartcards
Web: www.schlumberger.com

SECURITY ENGINEERED MACHINERY CO. INC
5 Walkup Dr. P.O. Box 1045
Westboro, MA 01581
Contact: Leonard Rosen, C.E.O.
Tel: (508) 366-1488 x 237
Fax: (508) 366-6814
E-mail: info@sernshred.com

SIEMENS NIXDORF INFORMATION SYSTEM INC.
Manufacturer Beetle 3/ 60, a 386SR based POS terminal using MS/DOS or Unix operating system
6400 Shafer Ct.
Rosemount, IL 60018
Contact: Dan Meeks, Division of Marketing Manager
Tel: (708) 698-0300
Fax: (708) 698-6089

SIGNATURE CARD INC.
Card Service
2526 Manana Drive
Suite 203-A
Dallas, TX 75220
Tel: (214) 358-8600
Fax: (214) 366-0911
E-mail: bobby@ signaturecard.net
Web: www.signaturecard.net

SMITH BARNEY, INC.
Investment Bank with focus on the credit card industry
388 Greenwich Street
New York, NY 10013
Contact: Hans Morris, Managing Director
Tel: (212) 816-8173
Fax: (212) 816-7087

SODEXHO MARRIOTT SERVICES
Food services
9801 Washington Blvd.
Gaithersburg, MD 20878
Contact: Ed Anderson
Tel: 301-987-4214
www.sodexhomarriott.com

SOUTHERN DATACOMM INC.
POS Terminal Services
19345 US Highway 19 North, Suite 200
Clearwater, FL 34624
Contact: Gary Eng, President
Tel: (813) 539-1800
Fax: (813) 535-7971

SPENCER ZAHN
& ASSOCIATES
Advertising
2015 Sansom Street
Philadelphia, PA 19103
Tel: (215) 564-5979
Fax: (215) 564-6285

STARK/LIVINGSTON, INC.
Research, consulting, and communications
Product Development
66 Oak Creek Trail
Madison, WI 53717-1610
Contact: Peter Livingston
Tel: (608) 833-5235
Fax: (608) 833-1045
E-mail: plivingston@mailbag.com

STA TRAVEL, INC.
Provides Student Travel Service
5900 Wilshire Blvd., Ste. 2110
Los Angeles, CA 90036
Contact: Andria Piekarz
Tel: (213) 937-1150 x 810
Fax: (213) 937-2739

STUDENT ADVANTAGE
SA Cash Program, marketing campus cards
Nationwide to off-campus merchants
University Business Unit
280 Summer Street
Boston, MA 02210-1131
Contact: Frederick Rogers, Vice President
Tel: (617) 912-2038
Fax: 617-257-0642
E-mail: fred@studentadvantage.com
Web: www.studentadvantage.com

STUDIOSMITH
Graphic Design
830 S. Ottillia S.E.
Grand Rapids, MI 49507
Tel: (616) 248-5339
Fax: (616) 248-4415
E-mail: barry@studiosmith.com
Web: www.studiosmith.com

SUNTRONIC TECHNOLOGY GROUP
Manufacturer of Suntronic POS systems
6711 Sands Rd.
Crystal Lake, IL 60018
Contact: Michael P. Nicolas
Tel: (815) 459-1959
Fax: (815) 455-1478

THE SUPPLY DEPARTMENT
POS Terminal Services
432 S. 22nd St.
Heath, OH 43056
Contact: Biff Matthews, President
Tel: (614) 522-2150
Fax: (614) 345-1985

SUPPLY EXPRESS INC.
POS Terminal Services
8868 Clairemont Mesa Blvd. Suite A
San Diego, CA 92123
Contact: Bart Thompson, President
Tel: (619) 492-8350
Fax: (619) 492-1097

SWIDLER BERLING SHEREFF
FRIENDMAN, LLP
Professional Services Legal/ Patent
The Chrysler Building
405 Lexington Ave
New York, NY 10174 USA
Tel: (212) 9730111
E-mail. Mfornes@sct.ictnet.es

TCF BANK
405 East Main Street
Anoka, MN 55303
Contact: Viane Hoefs, Manager, Campus Card Programs
Tel: 612-323-2935
E-mail: vhoefs@mailbox.tcfbank.com

TELECOM BUSINESS SERVICES
POS Terminal Services
1535 E. Orangewood Ave., Suite 107
Anaheim, CA 92805
Contact: Clive Buckley, President
Tel: (800) 827-9941
Fax: (714) 978-9946

TELEPRINT USA INC.
Card services
220 Business Center Drive
Reisterstown, MD 21136
Tel: (410) 526-1797
Fax: (410) 526-1799
E-mail: teleprint@worldnet.att.net

TESA ENTRY SYSTEMS, INC.
Establishing Business Partnerships, Electronic Locking Systems, Electronic Master Keying Systems, Campus Security
2100A Nancy Hanks Dr.
Norcross, GA 30071
Contact: Mark Doi, Education Market Representative
Tel: 770-447-4105
Web: www.tesalocks.com

TOKHEIM CORP.
Provides Spectra PC- based POS systems for C-stores and fueling stations
P.O.Box 360
Fort Wayne, IN 46801
Contact: Doug Currie, Director, System Marketing & Engineering
Tel: (219) 470-4600
Fax: (219) 471-2001

TOUCH TECHNOLOGY INTERNATIONAL
2201 E. Camelback Rd., Ste. 300B
Phoenix, AZ 85016
Contact: Steve Smith, V.P. Product Marketing
Tel: (602) 954-4805
Fax: (602) 954-6127
E-mail: ssmith@touchtechnology.com

TRITON SYSTEM INC.
Manufactures POS equipment
522 E. Railroad St.
Long Beach, MS 39560
Contact: Ernest L. Burdette, President
Tel: (601) 868-1317
Fax: (601) 868 –0437

U.S. WIRELESS DATA INC.
Manufactures POS eqipment
4888 Pearl E. Circle, # 110
Boulder, CO 80301
Contact: Alan B. Robert, President an CEO
Tel: (303) 440-5464
Fax: (303) 440-5640

VERIFONE
Pos Terminals
4988 Great America Parkway
Santa Clara, CA 95054 USA
Tel: (408) 919-4550
Fax: (408) 919-8903
E-mail: noel_b1@verfone.com
Web: www.verfone.com

VINGCARD PERSONA
Worldwide management, Manufacturer of offline electromechanical locking systems, Campus Environment
9333 Forest Lane
Dallas, TX 75243
Contact: Felix Mira, Vice President of VingCard PERSONA Division
Tel: 800-225-8464, x338
E-mail: fmira@vingcardpersona.com
www.vingcard-usa.com

WACHOVIA
100 N. Main St.
Winston-Salem, NC 27150
Contact: Tambra Nichols, A.V.P.
Tel: (910) 732-2019
Fax: (910) 732-2604
E-mail: morrcc68@aol.com

WALLACE'S BOOKSTORES, INC
Offers an innovative approach to college and university bookstores management
928 Nandino Blvd.
Lexington, KY 40512-1039
Contact: Tim Prather, Vice President of Marketing and Development
Tel: (606) 254-8861
Fax: (606) 254-9292
E-mail: tprather@compuserve.com
Web: www.wallaces.com

WEB SERVICE CO, INC.
Provides convenient, attractive, trouble-free laundry rooms with commissions.
3690 Redondo Beach Ave
Redondo Beach, CA 90278
Contact: David Kent, Sr
Tel: (800) 421-6897 x 634
Fax: (909) 899 –1459
E-mail: dryerman@aol.com

WELLS FARGO
Student Financial Services
2200 John Glenn Drive
Concord, CA 94520
Contact: Darrell Coleman, VP & Marketing Manager
Tel: 925-686-7825
www.wellsfargo.com

WILDEN PLASTICS (USA)
Provide Molded CardsWith or Without a Chip Pocket
650 Highway 74 South
Peachtree City, GA 30269
Contact: Jeff Nielsen
Tel. (770) 631-4939
Fax. (770) 631-0724
E-Mail: jnielsen@wilden.com

WILLIAM EXLINE, INC.
12301 Bennington Ave.
Cleveland, OH 44135
Contact: William Exline, President
Tel: 216-941-0800
E-mail: Williamexline@multiverse.com

W.T. BERESFORD COMPANY
26400 Lahser Rd. Ste. 308
Southfield, MI 48034
Contact: Tom Beresford, Asst. Vice President
Tel: (248) 350-2900
Fax: (248) 350-3115

WILLIAM EXLINE COMPANY
12301 Bennington Ave.
Cleveland, OH 44135
Contact: William B. Exline, President
Tel: 216-941-0800
Fax: 216-941-4885

Z-TEL COMMUNICATIONS, INC.
10240 Fimple Road
Chico, CA 95928
Contact: Keith Franco, Pacific Sales
Tel: 813-262-3447
Fax: 530-345-9098
E-mail: kfranco@z-tel.com